# *Good News for All*

## THE GOSPEL OF LUKE

Resource Book

**Carol J. Miller**

## *the* KERYGMA *program*

Art and Layout: Kathy Boykowycz

Grateful acknowledgement is hereby made for permission to include quotations from the *New Revised Standard Version Bible*, copyright 1989, Division of Christian Education of the National Council of Churches of Christ in the United States of America.

*Good News for All: The Gospel of Luke* is published and distributed by The Kerygma Program, Suite 205, 300 Mt. Lebanon Boulevard, Pittsburgh, PA 15234. Phone: 800/537-9462 FAX: 412/344-1823.

ISBN 1-882236-28-9

Kerygma on the Web: www.kerygma.com

Suite 205, 300 Mt. Lebanon Boulevard, Pittsburgh, Pennsylvania 15234

# CONTENTS

# *Foreword*

The Gospel according to Luke is without doubt one of the most valuable of all the basic documents of the Christian faith. Each New Testament author adds more to our picture of Jesus, and therefore, to our picture of the nature of God. Luke's contribution is a major one. How much poorer would our understanding of the love of God be without the parables of the Searching Woman or the Lost Sons? It is in Luke that we are brought up against ourselves in the parables of the Rich Fool, and the Rich Man and Lazarus. Thanks to Luke's love of God and of the Christian community we have been given a clear picture of Jesus as the one who cares about the poor and about those whom first century (and twentieth century) people saw as second class. It is Luke who shows us a Savior whose love reaches around the world, who breaks the bonds of race and nation. And it is Luke who points us to the power of prayer and of the Holy Spirit in Jesus' life. In the book of Acts these same themes will be developed by Luke as they are made manifest in the life of the Christian community.

## The Approach of this Study

In this study we will usually approach the material in the order in which Luke has written it. It will become apparent quite early that Luke arranged the material he had in very specific ways and for specific reasons. His tactic of using contrasting pairs of stories throughout the Gospel keeps the reader from sliding into an easy dogmatism. There are a few exceptions to our approach. The most notable is in Part 4, where we look at the exorcisms and other healings Jesus performed. Since such episodes are scattered throughout Jesus' ministry, I thought it best to group them here and deal with them all at once.

My work is based on the study of Luke's Gospel by Dr. Fred B. Craddock in the Interpretation series. In fact, at many points this book is closely informed by Dr. Craddock's perspective. For example, Dr. Craddock is concerned with being sensitive to Luke's arrangement of the material. That is because Luke is more than a chronicler. Luke is a theologian who writes from a faith perspective to show us the truth that lies in the depths of Jesus' words and actions. Dr. Craddock is also concerned to make the reader aware of the ties to the Hebrew Scriptures that are woven through Luke's work. So, whatever fresh insights are provided by my book most likely came from the mind and writing of Dr. Craddock.

A point of departure from Dr. Craddock's work, however, comes in the interpretation of some of the parables. In these instances I was drawn to the work of Dr. Kenneth Bailey, who has looked at the parables of Jesus through the eyes of the Palestinian peasants who heard them first. Dr. Bailey is in a unique position to do this since he has spent many years living in a Middle-Eastern culture, which he contends has changed little since the time of Jesus. For many years, he was Professor of New Testament at the Near East School of Theology, Beirut, Lebanon. In examining the parables of the Great Dinner, the Rich Fool, and the Lost Sons, I have followed Dr. Bailey's closely-worked interpretations rather fully. There are several benefits to this: the meaning of Jesus' parables becomes clear and sometimes startlingly fresh; we are shown how the original audience and the culture out of which the stories come are critical to interpreting the parables; and we are warned against taking such material and assuming that we can simply apply modern western understandings to it.

## *Preparing for the Group Sessions*

The study you are undertaking is a thorough overview of one of the most important books of the Bible. Therefore, it will be helpful for you to approach the work you are about to do in a systematic way. I suggest the following process.

1. Obtain a good study Bible with notes and cross references for each section of the text. This will be the major resource for your study. Several are available, including the *New Oxford Annotated Bible with Apocrypha (NRSV), The Oxford Study Bible with Apocrypha, and the New Jerusalem Bible.* (The *New Revised Standard Version* is the translation on which this course is based. Quotations of the biblical text are from this version and are printed in *italics*. However, you will be able to engage in the study effectively with another translation.)

2. Read the entire Gospel of Luke before you begin. Discover the rhythm of the book. Be alert to those themes and people that occur again and again. Watch how Jesus deals with different individuals and groups.

3. Review the format of this *Resource Book*. Note that each chapter begins with a **Summary**. The **Basic Bible References** for the chapter follow. These passages are the primary ones you should read to prepare for the group session. They are printed in bold type in the text. Many other references will also be listed in the text. They will help to reinforce, elaborate or explain the subject being considered. A **Word List** containing terms or phrases from the Bible references or this *Resource Book* which may be new to you is also included.

   At the end of each chapter you will find several items **For Further Study and Reflection**. The first section recommends texts to be included in your "Memory Bank." These are familiar passages that are so central to knowledge of the Bible that you should be able to recall their content or to recite them. The second section suggests "Research" projects which will enrich your grasp of the material, but are not essential. Lastly, there are comments and questions for "Reflection" which will challenge you to explore further the issues raised in the chapter.

4. When you are dealing with a particular part in the *Resource Book*, read all the Basic Bible References before you begin. Then read them again when they come up in the body of the text. You will need to keep the Gospel of Luke open before you as you study. Also be aware of the items in the Word List, making sure that you discover in the text the meaning of any unfamiliar word or phrase.

5. Keep an open mind. Do not let the familiarity of a story or saying make you skip over the discussion. Try to come to the study with an eagerness to hear what the text has to say, even if it may say something quite different than you expected.

6. Be alert to what the Gospel of Luke has to say for us today and for the world in which we live. The Scriptures deal with human beings and their relationship to God. These are constants in all times and places.

7. Surround your study with prayer. Pray before you begin and when you have finished a part. Ask for guidance; ask for a deeper knowledge of God and therefore a deeper knowledge of yourself. Ask also for the strength to act as Christ calls you to act.

### *Introducing the Rev. Dr. Carol Jean Miller*

Dr. Miller is an ordained elder in the United Methodist Church. The recipient of several academic honors, she earned the B.A. degree from Illinois Wesleyan University and M.Th. and D.Min. degrees from Perkins School of Theology, Southern Methodist University. For the last twenty-six years she has been in pastoral ministry, serving churches in Arkansas, Texas, Pennsylvania and Wisconsin. She is currently Pastor of Memorial United Methodist Church in Greenfield, Wisconsin.

Dr. Miller and her husband Richard have two daughters. As this volume goes to press Heather is beginning a time of service with the Peace Corps as an elementary teacher in Lesotho, Africa. Mary is a sophomore at Emory University.

During the last fifteen years, Dr. Miller has written numerous articles and curriculum materials for the United Methodist Publishing House. Her specialty is adult education, but she has authored publications for all age groups from elementary students to senior high youth. She has written both the *Resource Book* and the *Leader's Guide* for *Good News for All: The Gospel of Luke*.

## SUMMARY

Luke tells us that from many sources, written and oral, he has put together an orderly account. No careful author includes all the material at hand. Decisions must be made about what to include and what to exclude. Luke's audience, the times, and Luke's major interests all were factors in determining what he selected. His audience quite probably included Gentiles well versed in the Old Testament. His times were the turbulent years following the Fall of Jerusalem. His interests were many. Those to be explored here are: the universality of the gospel; social relationships between rich and poor; concern for outcasts, sinners, and Samaritans; women; the role of prayer, especially Jesus' prayers; the role of the Holy Spirit; the fulfillment of the Old Covenant; and the cost of discipleship. This introductory session will help us understand the rest of our study.

## BASIC BIBLE REFERENCES

Luke, chapters 1-24, especially 1:1-4

## WORD LIST

Q source
L source
canonized
Theophilus
God-fearer
universality

# Getting Started
# with Luke

## Luke Writes an Orderly Account

Moslem tradition teaches that the holy book, the *Koran*, was dictated by Allah directly to Mohammed, who dictated it to scribes. The book, therefore, supposedly contained no human influence or errors. It was, quite literally, the words of Allah. The Gospel of Luke was written in quite a different way. In the opening sentences of his book, Luke explains the way his Gospel came to be: read **1:1-4**. First Luke lists the sources that were available to him when he sat down to write. There were already in existence: 1) many *orderly accounts* and 2) the testimony of *eyewitnesses and servants of the word*. Armed with these, Luke tells us that he investigated *everything carefully from the very first* in order to write one more *orderly account*.

## Sources

Many questions have been asked over the years about who the eyewitnesses, the report writers, and the preachers were to whom Luke refers in 1:1-4. Several theories have been advanced. One of the most widely held theories states that Luke and Matthew are built primarily on the Gospel of Mark. Over three hundred verses of Luke's Gospel are the same as verses in the Gospel of Mark. In addition, many scholars believe that Luke had another written source which Matthew also used. This is referred to as the "Q" source after the German word *quelle*, which means "source." Q would have been a collection of Jesus' teachings containing few, if any, narratives and no story of Jesus' passion. This written source no longer exists except as it has been preserved in Luke and Matthew. These Gospels share over two hundred verses from this source. This material is found in more scattered form in Luke than in Matthew.

Luke's narratives about Jesus' birth and infancy, along with the parables of the Prodigal Son and the Good Samaritan, are some of the 582 verses unique to Luke. This material probably came from a source not available to the other Gospel writers. (Scholars refer to this as the "L" or Lukan source. John's Gospel was probably not yet written. There may well have been other collections from which Luke could have used material, but they are no longer in existence.)

It is clear from Luke's prologue that he himself is not an eyewitness to the life of Jesus. If he had been, he certainly would have made that fact the basis of his authority. But he claims to have firsthand accounts from those who had been closest to Jesus. We cannot know who his *eyewitnesses* were or if they were members of Jesus' inner circle. However, when we read, *But Mary treasured all these words and pondered them in her heart* (2:19), and *His mother treasured all these things in her heart* (2:51b), we can ask, "How does Luke know that?" We remember that he *investigated everything* and then *carefully* chose the sayings, incidents, and stories from which he would construct his *orderly account*.

## Inspiration

So Luke compiled his material himself, picking and choosing what to include. As far as Luke is concerned, then, inspiration is not infallible dictation from God to a human writer. Rather, the writer is deeply involved in gathering and shaping the material that he believes to be important, and he presents this material in a form that is helpful to his particular audience. After reading Luke's Gospel, however, no one would doubt that Luke had a deep, personal relationship with Christ. He is inspired by God to share with his readers that experience and the experiences of others.

Luke's hope is that his audience, having read about Jesus, will come to a firsthand experience of Christ. Luke's expectations must have been much the same as John's, who wrote: *But these are written so that you may come to believe that Jesus is the Messiah, the Son of God, and that through believing you may have life in his name* (John 20:31).

## Authority

The Gospels became authoritative for the Christian community when the community itself came to cherish these writings. In them the people met God revealed in Christ. Writings such as Luke's Gospel were treated as highly important from the first. As early as A.D. 150

leaders of the Christian church began to quote from works such as Matthew and Luke as sources of authority. Early church liturgies also quoted from some of the writings, including Luke. Slowly lists of writings deemed to be authoritative for the church began to emerge. Luke's Gospel was always on these lists. The New Testament as we have it now was not canonized, that is accepted as a uniquely authoritative collection, until A.D. 367. But there was never any doubt in the Christian communities that Luke's Gospel was authoritative.

No leaders or formal lists of books can make the Scriptures authoritative for an individual. The books of the Bible become authoritative for us or for any Christian community when they open a door to God. It is when we, reading Scripture, can say, "Yes, that is the God I have met firsthand," that Scripture becomes authoritative. Our experience of God at work in our own lives authenticates the Scriptures for us.

## *Date*

Luke often dates the events in his work by naming the Roman and Jewish leaders in power at the time. (See 1:5; 2:1-2 for examples.) Unfortunately, he does not tell us when he wrote the Gospel. Although some disagree about dates, we will probably not go far wrong with a date of A.D. 80-90. This places the writing of the Gospel after the Fall of Jerusalem and the destruction of the Temple (A.D. 70). Persecutions by the Romans are beginning. The Gospel is moving far beyond the confines of Israel and of Judaism. Gentiles are joining the church in large numbers. As you read Luke try to imagine what his readers may have been going through.

## *Authorship*

Nowhere in the third Gospel is Luke named as the author. The title was not part of the original document. But church tradition has always attributed the Gospel to Luke *the beloved physician* mentioned by Paul (Colossians 4:14; also see Philemon 1:24 and 2 Timothy 4:11). Fortunately, proving the identity of the author is not essential to understanding the Gospel. Knowing Luke's name does not tell us much more about the writer.

We know for certain that the author of Luke's Gospel also wrote the Acts of the Apostles. We have, in fact, a two-volume work. Compare Luke 1:1-4 with Acts 1:1-2. There are many other clues, such as shared vocabulary, sentence structure, and themes, which make it possible to say definitely that Luke and Acts are by the same hand. Together Luke/Acts constitutes the largest body of writing by one person in the New Testament, one-fourth of the total.

## The Need to Be Selective

Try to imagine a book that recorded a person's every word and every action for a year. Even if the book included only significant conversations and events, it would be a very large volume. It is obvious that none of the four Gospels attempts to record every word and action of Jesus. John says as much at the end of his Gospel: *But there are also many other things that Jesus did; if every one of them were written down, I suppose that the world itself could not contain the books that would be written* (21:25). The Gospel writers, therefore, had to choose what they would include and what they would leave out.

## Criteria for Selection: Audience

One of the deciding factors in what should be included in a work is the needs and interests of the audience to which the author is writing. For example, a Gospel writer who was addressing poor people would be careful to include many of Jesus' words that give hope to the destitute. Or the author might be careful to explain customs to readers unfamiliar with the culture. Luke certainly had to keep his audience in mind.

Luke addresses his work to the *most excellent Theophilus*, a Greek name which means "friend of God." We cannot know for certain, however, that this man was Greek, for many Jews, especially those living outside Israel, had Greek names. He may have been a man of social position as the words *most excellent* can imply. We do not know whether he was a Christian, a Jew, or a pagan. Although he appears to be a particular individual, Luke could be addressing his work to any "friend of God."

Traditionally, Luke's Gospel has been thought of as the Gospel to the Gentiles (non-Jews). The book contains numerous stories and sayings of Jesus that put Gentiles in a favorable light. The parable of the Good Samaritan (10:25-37), found only in Luke, is perhaps the most notable example. There are places in Matthew, written to a Jewish audience, which use the words *tax collectors and Gentiles* as a way of saying "sinners," but Luke writes *tax collectors and sinners* in those contexts. Matthew may have been using an expression common among Jews, without concern for what Gentiles might think, while Luke changes the language to avoid alienating a Gentile audience.

If Luke is writing to a Gentile audience, it is almost certainly an audience that knows the Hebrew Scriptures and considers those Scriptures to be authoritative. For while Luke only occasionally quotes directly from the Old Testament, his allusions to it are numerous. These could be picked out only by persons familiar with the Jewish Scriptures. In addition, Luke is careful from the beginning of the Gospel to its end to show the reader how the covenant promises of the Old Testament find their fulfillment in Jesus. Only those for whom the Old

Testament was authoritative would find this significant. In the first century there were many non-Jews who held to the Jewish Scriptures. They were called "God-fearers," Gentiles who worshiped the God of Israel but had not yet become converts to Judaism. The centurion of 7:1-10 may have been a "God-fearer." (See also Luke's description of Cornelius in Acts 10:1-2.).

## Criteria for Selection: Major Interests of Luke

Another factor which determines how an author selects material is the major interests of the individual writer. Luke has particular reasons for writing his Gospel. The orderly accounts already in existence were not sufficient for his purpose. Scholars have devised many lists of Luke's major interests. We shall now look at some of the themes that are most pervasive and shall give examples from the text.

### Universality

Luke is concerned to show that the gospel of Jesus Christ is for all people of all nations. He traces Jesus' genealogy back not only to Abraham, as Matthew does, but to Adam, the ancestor of all people (3:38). In 2:32 Simeon prophesies concerning the work of Jesus and announces that he will be *a light for revelation to the Gentiles* … In 4:25-27 the congregation at the synagogue in Nazareth attempts to kill Jesus when he reminds them that at difficult times in Israel's past history Elijah and Elisha were sent to help Gentiles. The parable of the Great Dinner (14:15-24) implies that if the people of Israel decline the invitation to feast in the kingdom of God, God's servants will *go out into the roads and lanes* to invite in those beyond the nation of Israel.

### Social relationships between the rich and poor

Luke's Gospel has been called the Gospel to the poor. In it we find numerous messages to and about the poor and the social nobodies. In 6:24-26 a list of "woes" follows the beatitudes and includes *woe to you who are rich, for you have received your consolation.* The parable of the Rich Fool (12:13-21) is unique to Luke, as is the parable of the Rich Man and Lazarus (16:19-31). Both are stories that condemn the greedy. The story of Zacchaeus, who is converted from his greed, is found exclusively in Luke (19:1-10).

### Concern for outcasts, sinners, and Samaritans

This Gospel abounds with stories of the forgiving of sinners (7:36-50; 15:1-32; 19:1-10), the healing and acceptance of outcasts (4:31-37; 5:12-13; 9:37-43), and the commending of Samaritans (10:25-37; 17:11-19). It is clear in Luke that these misfits and nobodies are precisely people for whom Jesus came.

## Women

Women play a much more prominent role in Luke than in the other Gospels. The birth narrative is told from Mary's point of view. Elizabeth is the first to call Jesus *Lord* (1:43). Anna the prophetess witnesses Jesus' presentation in the Temple (2:36-38). Luke also tells of the widow at Nain (7:11-17), the penitent sinner (7:36-50), and many women from Galilee who provide funds for Jesus and the Twelve (8:1-3). A woman is found representing God in the parable of the Lost Coin (15:8-10) and being the "hero" of the parable of the Widow and the Unjust Judge (18:1-8).

## The role of prayer, especially Jesus' prayers

Luke understands the parables of the Friend at Midnight (11:5-13) and the Widow and the Unjust Judge (18:1-8) to be about persistence in prayer. At all the great moments of Jesus' life, Luke shows him at prayer: at his baptism (3:21-22), before he calls the disciples (6:12), before he predicts his death (9:18), at the Transfiguration (9:28-36), and on the cross (23:46).

## The role of the Holy Spirit

Luke and Acts could well be called "the Acts of the Holy Spirit." At every significant point Luke reminds us that power comes from the Holy Spirit. Jesus will be born by the power of the Holy Spirit (1:35); Elizabeth, Zechariah, Simeon, and Anna all prophesy by the Holy Spirit; the Holy Spirit descends upon Jesus after his baptism (3:21-22) and he begins his work. In the synagogue at Nazareth Jesus reads from Isaiah, *The Spirit of the Lord is upon me …* (4:18a). From the time of Jesus' baptism through the end of the Gospel of Luke the Holy Spirit resides wholly in Jesus. At Pentecost the Holy Spirit fills the Christian community (Acts 2:1-4).

## The Old Covenant fulfilled

For Luke the promises of God are all coming true in Jesus. Mary's song (1:54-55) declares that in Jesus God is remembering all the promises made to Abraham and his descendants. Zechariah prophecies in the same way: *Thus he has shown the mercy promised to our ancestors, and has remembered his holy covenant, the oath that he swore to our ancestor Abraham …* (1:72-73a). Jesus is recognized by Peter and others as the promised Messiah (9:20).

*The cost of discipleship*

Again and again Jesus reminds his followers and would-be followers that to be his disciples will cost them everything. See the call of Peter (5:10-11), making the good confession before the authorities (12:4-12), warning about carrying the cross (14:25-33). The call to discipleship is a radical call. Before answering the call of Christ, people are warned to count the cost.

Each of these themes recurs throughout the Gospel. We will explore them more fully at various points during the next several sessions. Be alert to them as you read Luke's Gospel.

## *Organization of the Gospel of Luke*

Luke organized in a coherent fashion the materials he had chosen for his Gospel. Here is a brief outline of that organization:

I    Preface, 1:1-4

II    Birth and infancy narratives, 1:5-2:52

III    Ministry in Galilee, 3:1-9:50

IV    The journey through Samaria to Jerusalem, 9:51-19:27

V    Jerusalem ministry, 19:28-21:38

VI    The passion and resurrection narratives, 22:1-24:53.

Skim through each of the six sections to get an overview of what material is contained in each part. If your Bible has headings, use those. Then read the Gospel of Luke at one sitting. Luke intended this Gospel about Jesus to be a fascinating whole.

**FOR FURTHER STUDY AND REFLECTION**

**Memory Bank**

Memorize 1:1-4 as a reminder of how Luke put his Gospel together.

**Research**

1. Choose one of Luke's eight "criteria for selection" and follow the theme through the Gospel. It may be helpful to use a concordance to find all the references to the topic you have chosen (for example, "women" or "prayer").

2. Using a Bible dictionary, discover the meaning of the word "synoptic." What is the "synoptic problem"? (Your leader will help you find what Bible dictionaries are available.)

**Reflection**

1. Reread the sections titled "Inspiration" and "Authority." When did the Scriptures become authoritative for you?

2. What makes the Scriptures trustworthy? What would you say to someone who questioned the trustworthiness of the Gospels because of contradictions in them?

3. What is the proper role for the Scriptures? To what extent is it possible to make the Bible into an idol, into the thing in which you place your trust?

## SUMMARY

Luke's extensive birth narratives for both Jesus and John the Baptizer give important information concerning his understanding of Jesus' nature and significance. In the six songs or soliloquies offered by a variety of people and angels, Jesus' nature and mission are seen to be rooted deep in the covenant promises of the Old Testament. In this moving poetry, Luke looks back to Jesus' roots in the Old Testament and forward to Jesus' inauguration of the new age. Themes from the Old Testament are heard over and over. Lists of promises about to be fulfilled are recited. An understanding of these introductory chapters sharpens our senses to the main themes of the Gospel according to Luke.

## BASIC BIBLE REFERENCES

Luke 1:5-80
     2:1-52

## WORD LIST

Christology
Annunciation
angel
Messiah
eschatology
covenant

*2*

# God's Covenant Kept: Annunciations and Births

## Luke's Unique Material

The birth narratives that Luke records about John the Baptizer and Jesus are unique in the Gospels. Matthew and John make no mention of John's birth. Mark mentions neither birth. In the Gospel of John, the beautiful prologue (1:1-18) speaks of Jesus' coming in terms of the Word of God becoming flesh, but gives no account of the physical circumstances surrounding the birth. Matthew speaks of Jesus' birth, but tells of Magi from a foreign land and about the threat from Herod and the escape of Jesus and his family into Egypt (Matthew 2).

It is also only Luke who records the prophecies of Gabriel, Mary, Elizabeth and Zechariah. And, it is in Luke alone that Jesus' birth is announced by an angel chorus to shepherds. The material that Luke includes as he writes his *orderly account* is very deliberately chosen. What Luke places in the first two chapters of his Gospel contains the basis of Luke's Christology, that is, his belief about who Jesus Christ is. These accounts announce the purpose of Jesus' coming and his life and ministry.

There is a distinct pattern unfolding in these chapters. Two annunciations (announcements) are made by Gabriel; two births are recorded. These two sets of circumstances are tied together by the meeting of the two mothers-to-be. The story of Jesus continues in two scenes about the child Jesus in the Temple: one at six weeks of age, the other at twelve years. At every point in these events, the meaning is made clear by a song. These six songs or soliloquies make up a large part of the first two chapters.

## The Annunciations

Read **1:5-25**. The first announcement comes to Zechariah, Elizabeth's husband, as he performs his priestly duties in the Holy of Holies at the Temple in Jerusalem. He is confronted by the angel Gabriel. Gabriel is mentioned several times in the writings of late Judaism. Generally he is found delivering messages from God. The word "angel" comes from the Greek word for "messenger." Gabriel enumerates the functions that John is to perform for the Lord. John will cause *many of the people of Israel* to turn to God. By Elijah's prophetic powers John will go before the Messiah to make people ready to receive him. This is John the Baptizer's "job description." Many of the Jews who were waiting for the Messiah believed that Elijah, who was taken to heaven by God (2 Kings 2:11), would return as a forerunner of the Messiah (Malachi 4:5-6). "Messiah" is the Hebrew word for "anointed one." The equivalent word in Greek yields the term "Christ." The Holy Spirit is to be the source of John's prophetic message. Luke commonly reminds us that prophetic messages come not from the prophet alone, but are inspired by God's own Spirit.

Now read **1:26-38**. Gabriel makes several prophecies concerning Jesus. What will Mary's son be? In 2 Samuel 7:8-16, God promised David that he would always have a descendant on the throne of Israel. Be alert to see how in every announcement and song God's covenant relationship to Israel is remembered and its fulfillment assured. A covenant is a promise made between two or more parties. Luke 1:37 is a key affirmation of the Scriptures. These words spoken to Mary echo precisely the angelic visitor's question to Abraham concerning Sarah's forthcoming pregnancy (Genesis 18:14).

## The Barren Women

At several points in the Bible we see the motif of the barren woman who becomes pregnant to fulfill God's covenant: Sarah (Genesis 18:1-15), Rebekah (Genesis 25:21), Rachel (Genesis 30:1-2, 22-24), Hannah (1 Samuel 1:5, 19-20), and now Elizabeth. Sarah and Elizabeth were old women well past childbearing age. They were chosen to remind God's people that the future is a gift from God. It is not brought about by the manipulations of human beings. The history of God saving a people began with an elderly futureless couple, Abraham and Sarah, to whom God gave a future. The end of the story of salvation comes with an elderly barren couple whose child will announce the fulfillment of all God's promises. Mary, by contrast, is a young woman. Her son inaugurates the new age. Jesus' miraculous birth again reminds the reader that this is God's will and God's action in human history.

## The Visitation

On several occasions in Luke women make important pronouncements of God's will. Read **1:39-45**. Mary's visit to Elizabeth prompts Elizabeth's short but powerful speech and Mary's much longer song. Note that Elizabeth speaks in the power of the Holy Spirit. Elizabeth is the first to acknowledge Jesus as Lord (1:43), even before Jesus is born! Elizabeth praises Mary for her faith: she trusts God's word. Such trust has been the hallmark of God's people from the very beginning of the salvation story (see Genesis 15:6).

Now turn to **1:46-56**. Mary's song, often called the *Magnificat* from the first word of the song in Latin, is important for understanding the reason for Jesus' coming. This song is strongly reminiscent of Hannah's song in 1 Samuel 2:1-10. Mary blesses God's goodness to her and to all people who honor God across the centuries. What God has done for Mary is representative of what God will do for all the poor–lift up the lowly.

Mary rejoices in the meaning of God's present action, the coming of Jesus. However, it is interesting to note how she links her praise to the actions of God in the past. The mighty works of God, which have been present throughout Israel's history, are here celebrated as being assured for the future: *He has helped his servant Israel, in remembrance of his mercy, according to the promise he made to our ancestors, to Abraham and to his descendants forever.* Jesus is the fulfillment of the covenant promise. The announcement of Jesus' coming guarantees that all the promises of God are coming true; in fact they are as good as done! Mary can speak of them as if they have already happened.

Verses 52-53 are central to Luke's message. This has been called the classical statement of God's activity. The theme of God's reversal of all human structures will remain pivotal throughout Luke's Gospel. The Final Judgment is anticipated in these verses.

## Zechariah's Song

As Mary awaits the birth of her son, the scene shifts to the birth of John. Read **1:57-80**. Zechariah, his tongue loosened by God, speaks by the power of the Holy Spirit. Although this is the scene where John should be central, verses 68-75 speak not of John but of Jesus. There can be absolutely no doubt that for Luke, who chose to relate these particular events, Jesus is the fulfillment of the Old Testament covenant. Jesus is Judaism's hope fulfilled. Zechariah's song echoes Mary's statements about the final fulfillment of God's will. This looking ahead to the consummation of history and to the end time is called "eschatology." We will see throughout Luke's Gospel how Jesus' life, teaching, death, and resurrection speak about the "eschaton," the completion of history, when God's will is done fully and

God reigns in every heart. The meaning of Jesus' coming is found in the promises of the Old Testament.

John's job description is to get the people ready to receive their Savior. It is no surprise that in liturgical churches John's preaching is read during the Advent season. The summary, not only of John's message but also of Jesus', is put into one sentence: ... *you will go before the Lord to prepare his ways, to give knowledge of salvation to his people by the forgiveness of their sins* (verses 76b-77).

The last two verses of Zechariah's song are a beautiful proclamation of the mercy and salvation of God. The poetry in these two chapters of Luke is exquisite. John now moves offstage and will not be seen again until, fully grown, he comes crashing out of the Judean wilderness to announce the Messiah's presence.

## The Birth of Jesus

Read **2:1-20**. There is no elaborate verbiage in Luke. Jesus' birth is recorded in one sentence. As a sign of the reversal of roles that the Messiah will bring, his birth is announced, not to kings and priests, but to shepherds, people considered unclean by Jewish law. It is to the no-accounts that the heavenly host proclaims its message because it is a message for the no-accounts. As Mary sang, *He has brought down the powerful from their thrones, and lifted up the lowly.*

The angel's message to the shepherds begins, as did the messages to Zechariah and Mary, *Do not be afraid.* The lowly, the humble, the no-accounts have nothing to fear. Note that it is the angel of God who gives Jesus the titles *Savior* and *Messiah.* There is no question as to Jesus' true role. The sign of the good news is a poor baby lying in a feed trough. Verse 14 is known as the *Gloria in Excelsis Deo* (Latin for "Glory to God in the highest"). The second half of the verse is difficult to translate. It may be rendered *on earth peace among those whom he favors,* meaning specific people. The more familiar "on earth peace, goodwill toward men" is the 1611 rendering of late medieval texts and suggests that God is pleased with all people–a kind of general amnesty. The heart of the angels' message is God's coming with peace, and the lowly of the earth should rejoice.

## The Presentation in the Temple

After the shepherds have left the manger *glorifying and praising God,* the scene changes again. Read **2:21-40**. Here we find the holy family in the Temple where Jesus' observant Jewish parents are doing all that the Law requires. They offer *two young pigeons,* the sacrifice acceptable for those who cannot afford a lamb. It should be noted that Luke has combined two different laws concerning childbirth: the purification of the mother (Leviticus 12:1-8) and the dedication of the firstborn son to God (Exodus 13:2, 12-16).

In the Temple the family meets elderly Simeon, who had been promised that he would not die before he had seen the Messiah. He recognizes the infant Jesus as the fulfillment of God's promise. His song is called the *Nunc Dimittis*, "now let your servant depart," the opening words of the song in Latin. These verses introduce another major theme of Luke's Gospel. Jesus will be *a light for revelation to the Gentiles.* Simeon is loosely quoting Isaiah 49:6b. Part of the reason for the covenant with Israel was to make Israel's faithfulness a beacon that would draw all the nations to worship Israel's God. Jesus, as the one who fulfills the covenant, is both the salvation of Israel and the salvation of the world. But Simeon also casts a shadow over the young family. The fulfilling of the covenant will not come without a price. *This child is destined for the falling and rising of many in Israel.* Controversy and the cross are overheard in this chilling prophecy. What is good news to the lowly will be perceived as a threat to the rich and powerful. Recall Mary's song in 1:51-53.

Anna, a prophetess and very elderly, does not have her words recorded. But Luke feels he must not fail to mention her. She thanks God and speaks about the child Jesus *to all who were looking for the redemption of Jerusalem.* Anna's message, too, is that Jesus is the Messiah for whom Israel has been waiting. Anna is the third woman of note in these two chapters. We see another of Luke's interests already taking shape.

## *Twelve-Year Old in the Temple*

The only other story in the Gospels regarding Jesus' childhood is found in **2:41-52**. Since Jesus is twelve years old, he would probably have become a *bar mitzvah*, "son of the commandment." The *bar mitzvah* is a ritual for Jewish boys performed at the age of twelve.[1] They are then considered adults, sons of the Law. They assume the responsibility and the privilege of keeping the Law of God. Hence, Jesus would be traveling to Jerusalem as an observant Jew. This incident portrays a touching mixture of a typical twelve-year-old boy who worries his parents without meaning to and the sensitive, insightful young man, not lecturing his elders but learning from them. The childhood narratives end with the gracious words: *And Jesus increased in wisdom and in years, and in divine and human favor.*

---

1   Today a Jewish girl becomes a *bat mitzvah*, "daughter of the commandment."

## FOR FURTHER STUDY AND REFLECTION

### Memory Bank

Memorize one or part of one of the songs studied in this session.

### Research

1. How is the angel's visit to Abraham and Sarah in Genesis 17:19-22; 18:9-15 similar to Gabriel's visit to Mary? In what ways are the visits different?

2. Compare Hannah's song in 1 Samuel 2:1-10 with Mary's song in Luke 1:46-55. What are the major themes in each song? How do they differ?

3. List the similarities in Mary's and Zechariah's songs.

### Reflection

1. Luke sees Jesus' birth as the fulfillment of the Old Testament covenant. What personal ties do you feel to the covenants of God with Abraham and with David?

2. Write a few lines of poetry putting into words the meaning of Jesus' coming for your life and the life of your faith community.

## SUMMARY

John comes crashing out of the Judean wilderness to announce the coming of God's Messiah. Luke presents John as the prophet who fulfills Isaiah's prophecy of a voice *crying out in the wilderness*. John is to announce that God's salvation is at hand, the salvation promised to the Jews. But ethnic heritage is no guarantee of acceptance by God. John offers a baptism that requires repentance and living an ethical life before God. In preparation for his ministry Jesus participates in this baptism, is filled with the Holy Spirit and heralded by God as God's own Son. Luke's genealogy of Jesus' ancestors then traces Jesus' antecedents back not only to Abraham but to Adam. The final preparation for Jesus' ministry is the Temptation. Jesus is tempted by physical needs, political power, and the desire to demand proofs from God. He rejects all of these temptations and returns to Galilee in the power of the Holy Spirit to begin the works of God.

## BASIC BIBLE REFERENCES

Luke 3:1-38
     4:1-13
     7:18-35
Hebrews 4:15
Deuteronomy 8:2, 3

## WORD LIST

Sanhedrin
high priest
repent
tax collector
epiphany
devil/Satan

*3*

# Preparations for Ministry

## Marking the Time

Begin your study by reading **3:1-2**. Typical of Luke, this introduction to Jesus' adult life begins with a dating of the events. The fifteenth year of Tiberius Caesar would be A.D. 28-29. Pontius Pilate, the procurator[1] of Judea, held his post from A.D. 26 to 36, when the Jews protested and he was replaced. After the death of Herod the Great, Herod's kingdom was divided into four parts or tetrarchys: Galilee, Iturea, Trachonitis, and Abilene. Luke uses the rulers of these territories to further expand on his dating. He also includes the rule of the high priests Annas and Caiaphas. High priests (also called chief priests) were the principal authorities in Judaism. Their influence was centered in the Temple and in the Sanhedrin, the seventy men who made up the highest court in Judaism. Although they were appointed for life, Rome tried to control their authority by deposing and appointing high priests at will. Annas was high priest from A.D. 6-15. Rome replaced him with his son-in-law Caiaphas who held the post until A.D. 36. The Jewish people still looked on Annas as high priest, so that even after Caiaphas was appointed Annas continued to have great influence. According to John 18:12-28, Jesus appeared before both at his trial. Having set Jesus' ministry in the context of both Jewish and Roman rulers, Luke brings us to the beginning of Jesus' work.

---

1   A procurator was a financial and/or military official who represented the Roman emperor either in Rome or in the provinces.

## The Prominence of John

Now read **3:3-6**. As in the birth narratives, stories about John precede those about Jesus. John fulfills Zechariah's prophecy about him (1:76-77). Luke identifies the mission of John with a prophecy from Isaiah (40:3-5). John is that voice *crying out in the wilderness*, the voice that announces the coming of the Lord into history and the fulfilling of all the promises to Israel.

This is not merely Luke's opinion of John. Read Luke **7:18-35**. In 7:27 Jesus confirms that John is the one of whom the scripture says: *See, I am sending my messenger ahead of you, who will prepare your way before you.* Jesus also testifies of John that he is a great prophet of Israel, and even more than a prophet. Jesus says, *I tell you, among those born of women no one is greater than John (7:28).* No one else comes anywhere near that kind of high praise from Jesus. In the Gospels John is the most frequently mentioned person after Jesus and Peter.

Luke introduces John with the traditional prophet's introduction, *The word of God came to John* (3:2b; see Jeremiah 1:2, Hosea 1:1, Joel 1:1 and Micah 1:1). The prophet does not speak his own message, but rather a message that has been given to him by God. Therefore, when a prophet speaks, God is speaking. Many of the common people were convinced by John's preaching that he was, indeed, a prophet (Luke 20:6). There had been no prophets in Israel for two hundred years. It is not surprising then that the people wonder whether John might be the Messiah (Luke 3:15).

## Baptism by John

Read **3:7-20**. The Jews of this time practiced baptism for those who were converted but not for those who were born into Judaism. John's baptism is different; he will accept for baptism only those who have shown by their actions that they have repented. The Old Testament word behind John's "repent" meant to "turn around." Luke uses a Greek word that means to "change one's mind." John insists that those coming to him make a complete change in the way they are living their lives and then demonstrate with actions that they have changed their thinking. The washing is symbolic of a life that has already begun to change. The actions must precede as well as follow the baptism: *Bear fruits worthy of repentance.*

John also ties his baptism to the imminent coming of the Messiah: *one who is more powerful than I is coming.* John describes the time of this coming as a time of judgment. A winnowing fork was used to throw grain into the wind where the chaff would be separated from the heavier kernel. John's description of the Messiah's coming sounds like the announcement of the Final Judgment. Perhaps that explains why later John sends messengers to ask

Jesus, *Are you the one who is to come, or are we to wait for another?* (Luke 7:19) For Jesus does not initiate the dramatic judgment that John seems to foresee. Rather, judgment comes as people and finally the nation accept or reject Jesus and his ministry.

Being born into God's people (descendants of Abraham) is no protection from God's wrath. Only deeds of compassion and justice will avail. There is no hand-me-down salvation in John's message. The actions that John demands are those of social justice. It is noteworthy that Jesus' ministry is prefaced by the social implications of the Gospel, one of Luke's major themes.

## God's Requirements

True repentance requires a change in one's relationships with others. It is marked by a changed relationship with the poor and suffering. Throughout Luke's Gospel we will see that sin is the breaking of a relationship with God. The symptoms of that brokenness are shattered relationships with others, especially those who need our help. Repentance, then, is the restoration of the relationship with God which produces healthy relationships between others and ourselves.

Two specific groups approach John to ask what true repentance will mean for them. Tax collectors were Jews who worked for the Romans and were therefore looked upon as traitors to Israel. They were allowed to take as much from the people as they could get, provided Rome got its share. John demands that tax collectors only collect what is owed, instead of becoming rich through extortion. Soldiers of the Roman occupation (Gentiles) also come for baptism and are instructed not to use threats of violence and blackmail to extort money from the peasants. Preparation for the Lord's coming consists of doing the works of justice and love. It is not surprising that the Advent season, the season of preparation for the Lord's coming, has traditionally been a time of helping the poor and showing concern for others. Lectionaries suggest that John's sermons be read on the second and third Sundays in Advent.

The last portion of John's message concerns his relationship to the Messiah. John himself had disciples, many of whom believed that John might be the long-awaited Messiah. This belief persisted even through the time of Jesus, and people continued to be baptized with John's baptism (see Acts 18:25 and 19:1-4). Luke, therefore, is careful to include the words of John concerning his relationship to God's Messiah. John distinguishes himself from the Messiah in three ways: 1) he is not worthy to be the Messiah's slave; 2) while John's baptism is with water to show repentance, the Messiah will baptize with the fire of the Holy Spirit of God; 3) the Messiah will pass judgment.

Luke finishes this section where John is prominent by including, almost as an aside, the arrest of John. This, however, did not happen until after the baptism of Jesus.

## The Baptism of Jesus

Read **3:21-22**. Since John's baptism was for repentance of sins, why was Jesus baptized? Luke makes no attempt to answer this question (but see Matthew 3:14-15). The early church was somewhat embarrassed by Jesus' baptism. This may be reflected in Luke's Gospel by the fact that Jesus' baptism is not described but only recorded. Luke focuses on the events that accompany the baptism and what they say about who Jesus is. While Jesus prays, the Holy Spirit descends on him and the voice of God assures Jesus that he is God's *Son, the Beloved*. The words are from Psalm 2:7, a psalm for the coronation of Israel's king. Luke sees in Jesus' baptism a demonstration of Jesus' divine Sonship. The baptism, then, is an "epiphany," a showing forth of God. From this moment on the Holy Spirit will speak uniquely through Jesus. As long as Jesus is on the earth, God's Spirit rests wholly in him. In Acts 2:4, after Jesus' ascension, the Holy Spirit rests on Jesus' gathered followers and they speak through the power of the Spirit.

Jesus' willingness to undergo John's baptism also lends authority to the ethical preaching of John. The reign of God is at hand. In God's kingdom love, mercy, and justice are the hallmarks of God's subjects. Following Jesus will mean the transformation of the whole basis from which a life is lived.

## The Genealogy of Jesus

At this point, Luke inserts a genealogy of Jesus. Read **3:23-38**. The only other such list of ancestors is found in Matthew 1:1-17. But while Matthew traces Jesus' lineage back as far as Abraham, Luke traces it back to the *son of Adam, son of God*. Luke's theme of universality again comes to the fore. All people are linked to Jesus and through Jesus to each other. The genealogy also serves to tie Jesus to Israel and to God's Old Testament promises to Israel. Jesus' lineage is through King David (3:31).

A comparison with Matthew's genealogy would show several differences in the names listed. It was not unusual to stylize a genealogy. Names were added or left out for a variety of reasons. Luke organizes Jesus' genealogy with eleven series of seven names each for a total of seventy-seven. Matthew sets up his genealogy to show three sets of fourteen generations each. The differences are not significant in locating Jesus in his proper lineage. Both genealogies fix Jesus firmly in Judaism.

Luke gives the reader one other valuable piece of information here. In 3:23 he states that *Jesus was about thirty years old when he began his work*. Only one other place in the New Testament mentions Jesus' age as an adult, John 8:57, and there the reference is vague.

## *The Temptation*

Temptations themselves are not signs of weakness, but of power. A person without the power to act cannot be tempted. Anyone with power, be it financial, political, or the power to influence a relationship, will review the possible ways that power might be used. Sin comes not in being tempted but in choosing to use the power available in a way displeasing to God. Read **Hebrews 4:15**. Jesus is called our *high priest* who *has been tested* but does not yield–*test* and *yield* both render the same word in the original text.

In Luke **4:1-13** Jesus is tempted precisely because he has the Holy Spirit's power. It is the Spirit that leads him into the desert to think about what he will do with this power. Jesus' temptations in the wilderness last forty days. Forty is an often-used number in the Scriptures. It indicates a significant period of time. Noah was in the ark forty days (Genesis 7:17). Moses was on the mountain for forty days and nights fasting while he received the Ten Commandments from God (Exodus 34:28). Jesus' time in the desert parallels the forty years the people of Israel were in the wilderness. Read **Deuteronomy 8:2, 3**. In fact, Jesus quotes from Deuteronomy 6 and 8 three times in the temptation narrative. Jesus has not been abandoned by God in the wilderness any more than the people of Israel were. But like those ancient Israelites, Jesus must make conscious decisions about his obedience to God.

Jesus is sent into the wilderness by God's Holy Spirit to make decisions about his use of power. He is tempted *by the devil*. The word "devil" means "slanderer" or "accuser" (derived from the Greek word *diabolos*; the word "satan" is a Hebrew derivative with the same meaning). Neither was originally a proper name. In the Old Testament they are not designations of a demonic power. "Satan" was originally a courtroom term (see Zechariah 3:1). By New Testament times the devil had become the seducer and tempter of humans, whose goal was to destroy people's relationship with God.[2]

Whether or not anyone observing this scene would have seen a second person with Jesus is not important for this discussion. A demonic influence need not present itself to us in physical form. This debate could well have taken place completely in the mind of Jesus, just as our temptations take place inside of ourselves. Certainly a demonic personage dressed in red tights and a tail would be too obvious to present much of a challenge (this concept of the devil is from the poet Dante, not from Scripture). Temptations are only

---

2   In Revelation 12:9, 10 all forces that oppose God are considered to be one.

tempting if they are dressed up as goodness, if they masquerade as an opportunity to use power for some righteous cause. Professor Craddock explains:

> … a real temptation is an offer not to fall but to rise. The tempter in Eden did not ask, "Do you wish to be a devil?" but, "Do you wish to be as God?" There is nothing here of debauchery; no self-respecting devil would approach a person with offers of personal, domestic, or social ruin. That is in the small print at the bottom of the temptation.[3]

Jesus is tempted in three ways. Each is an offer from the devil that Jesus counters with Scripture. It is important not to see this debate as a quick back-and-forth exchange of one-liners. Jesus spent forty days in the wilderness because the temptations to abuse his power were very compelling. There must have been a great struggle going on in his mind. His humanity is real, with all the difficulties which that entails. Jesus' answers represent a victory that has been hard won.

The first temptation is personal. Jesus is hungry and is tempted to use his power for his personal well-being. He is tempted to act as though his physical needs are the most important concern. This temptation to make physical needs the highest priority is common to us all. Jesus will address this concern in Luke 12:22-34 and in other of his teachings. This temptation may reflect a current messianic expectation as well. For several centuries the Jews had believed that when the Messiah came, he would usher in an era of unlimited prosperity.

> The time is surely coming, says the LORD,
>     when the one who plows shall overtake the one who reaps,
>     and the treader of grapes the one who sows the seed;
> the mountains shall drip sweet wine,
>     and all the hills shall flow with it. (Amos 9:13)

Jesus may have been tempted to fulfill popular messianic hopes, to be what the people expected him to be instead of what God wanted of him.

The second temptation is political. Jesus could rule the world by political manipulation, which would include control of the military. He could then force the kingdom of God. Again, the popular messianic expectations of Jesus' day may have been at work. Chief among the hopes for the Messiah was the desire to have him lead a revolt against Rome and restore Israel to the political greatness it had known a thousand years before under King David. This hope follows Jesus throughout the Gospel and even into Acts. At the time of his

---

3   Fred B. Craddock, *Luke*, Interpretation Series (Louisville:John Knox Press, 1990), p. 56.

Ascension, the disciples ask the risen Christ, *Lord, is this the time when you will restore the Kingdom to Israel?* (Acts 1:6). If Jesus would only worship the demonic–the power of violence, force and manipulation–what wonderful things he could do for Israel. Jesus refuses to compromise his loyalty to God and quotes Deuteronomy 6:13. Worship, then, includes giving oneself totally to the sources of power and the methods of the thing worshiped. The devil promises Jesus all the right outcomes if only he will use the tools of evil.

The third temptation is religious. The devil says *If you are the Son of God, throw yourself down from here.* How can Jesus know empirically that he has God's power, that he is God's Son? Maybe he is mistaken. If only he could have some hard evidence that God is with him, then this ministry that Jesus is facing would be much easier to bear. The devil's "if" is often heard by those who wonder whether God is really with them or not. It is here that the devil himself quotes Scripture (Psalms 91:11-12). This is the temptation to live not by faith, but by proof. And again, there may be a messianic overtone. There is a tradition of the rabbis that when the Messiah revealed himself, he would stand on the roof of the Temple. Perhaps Jesus is being tempted to prove to the people that he is the Messiah. Jesus counters with Deuteronomy 6:16. Even Jesus must trust where he cannot see. Jesus has chosen obedience to God; he has chosen to live a life that trusts only God.

Jesus needed to take a significant amount of time alone to pray and fast before he was ready to live for God. He had to consciously face temptations to misuse the abilities God had put into his hands. But, with the end of this section Jesus' temptations are not over. Luke tells us that the devil *departed from him until an opportune time.* The final temptation will come in the Garden of Gethsemane.

## FOR FURTHER STUDY AND REFLECTION

### Memory Bank

Memorize Jesus' answers to the devil's three temptations: Luke 4:4, 8, 12.

### Research

1. Read the parallels in Matthew, Mark, and John concerning the preaching of John the Baptizer. Also read an article on John in a Bible dictionary or other secondary resource. What new information about John do you glean from these readings?

2. Using a concordance, look up the references to John the Baptizer in Luke. How is he described? What is Jesus' opinion of him?

## Reflection

1. How might John the Baptizer answer if you asked him, "What must I do?"

2. What does it mean for you that Jesus was truly human, as Hebrews 4:15 says: *who in every respect has been tested as we are …?* How does it help your faith? How does it challenge your faith?

3. In what way are the three temptations of Jesus in Luke 4 similar to temptations you face? How do you respond to each kind of temptation?

## SUMMARY

Jesus begins his ministry in Galilee. His inaugural message, given at the synagogue in his hometown of Nazareth, outlines the purposes for which he came, but it also inflames nationalistic passions in his hearers. For the most part, however, Jesus' preaching in the synagogues of Galilee and his healing ministry are met with great enthusiasm by the common people. Jesus' preaching, teaching, and healing all serve to demonstrate that the reign of God is beginning in the here and now. Both men and women are called to accompany Jesus on his itinerant ministry. From among them twelve men are chosen as apostles and sent on a mission.

| BASIC BIBLE REFERENCES | WORD LIST |
|---|---|
| Luke 4:14-44 | exorcism |
| 5:1-32 | centurion |
| 6:12-16 | apostle |
| 7:1-17 | disciple |
| 8:1-3, 19-56 | zealot |
| 9:1-6, 37-43a, 49-50 | |
| 13:10-17 | |
| Leviticus 13:45-46 | |

*4*

*Jesus Inaugurates
the Kingdom
of God*

## Inauguration and Rejection

Read **4:14-30**. In a summary statement Luke very briefly informs the reader that Jesus is becoming well-known due to his extensive teaching in the synagogues throughout Galilee. He is being received with some enthusiasm. But Luke does not want to share the details of this teaching ministry before he has set before us Jesus' "inaugural" announcement, made in his home synagogue at Nazareth.

Luke first tells us that it was Jesus' custom to attend corporate worship in the synagogue. The synagogue service was rather informal. It was led by lay persons such as the Pharisees, and consisted mainly of prayers, Scripture reading, commenting on the Scripture, and receiving alms for the poor. Any adult male was welcome to read aloud the Scripture lesson for the day and then to comment on it. This is what Jesus is doing when he reads Isaiah 61:1-2.

Jesus uses this text to announce the purpose for his coming, and thereby the purpose of the faith community. He also uses the passage to define what he means by Messiah. His announcement is specific. The Messiah will: 1) bring good news to the poor; 2) proclaim liberty to the captives; 3) bring sight to the blind; 4) free the oppressed; 5) proclaim that God is saving his people now. In **4:42-44** Jesus reiterates his purpose to proclaim this *good news of the kingdom of God*.

The signs of God at work among the people of God are the good news of reconciliation, freedom, health, wholeness, and salvation. Jesus identifies himself as the one fulfilling this promise of God, which is nothing less than the reign of God beginning on earth. Everything that Jesus will do will signify the presence of God with the people of God. It will also define the life's work of Jesus' church. At Jesus' baptism God anointed him with "the spirit of the Lord." Later (in 7:18-23) when John the Baptizer sends messengers to ask if Jesus is the Messiah, Jesus will add even more to his description of the Messiah.

The congregation at Nazareth is quite impressed to hear *Joseph's son* ("Joe's boy"?) speaking so beautifully. But then Jesus reminds them that they will probably want him to do for them all they heard that he did at Capernaum, a town with a large Gentile population. Jesus defends his ministry beyond local and ethnic boundaries by reminding the people of two Old Testament stories where God's help came to Gentiles but not to the people of Israel. (You will find the backgrounds of the stories in 1 Kings 17:8-16 and 2 Kings 5:1-19). Among the Jews of Jesus' day there was an intense nationalism born of their chafing under Roman occupation. The popular concept of the Messiah was of one who would lead the revolt against the Gentile oppressors. Jesus makes it clear at the outset, by quoting their own Scriptures to them, that God is not limited by race and nation. Jesus has no intention of fulfilling the popular image of the Messiah. The people determine to destroy Jesus then and there, but he escapes, although Luke does not elaborate on how that is accomplished.

## The Disciples

Both Matthew and Mark place the call of the disciples much earlier than Luke does; they make it look as though it is simply Jesus' magnetic personality that causes the men to give up everything to join him. Turn to **5:1-11**. In Luke, Jesus has had a very popular teaching and healing ministry before he calls the disciples. Some of the disciples have witnessed Jesus' mighty acts; he has already healed Simon's mother-in-law. It thus seems a bit more natural that they would be ready to make such a dramatic shift in their lives.

The first call to discipleship comes when the press of the crowd leads Jesus to get into Simon's boat. (This incident is reminiscent of the resurrection appearance in John 21:1-14). The story centers on Simon Peter. Later (6:14) Luke will tell us that Jesus nicknamed Simon "Peter." The word is Greek for "rock" (in Hebrew *cephas*, the name Paul usually calls him), but Luke does not explain the nickname for us as the other Gospels do.

Professional fishermen on the Sea of Galilee, which Luke calls Lake Gennesaret, often fished through the night using large dragnets. The profession of fishing, along with that of shepherding, will become metaphors for the work Jesus' followers are to do. Jesus uses fishing in that way: ... *from now on you will be catching people.* Jesus' first definition of the role of his followers is to bring others to God. Simon Peter's partners are James and John, sons of Zebedee. This is our introduction to Jesus' closest companions. Peter, James, and John are the ones Jesus takes with him when others are not included (9:28).

The assumption in this story seems to be that these men, who know the lake as well as anyone, realize that the catch of fish described in 5:6-8 is not natural. To us it might be almost comic. Simon tiredly tells the landlubber Jesus that there are no fish around, but throws out the nets anyway. And immediately there is a fish frenzy, fish everywhere, breaking the nets by the sheer weight of them; filling two boats, both boats so loaded with fish that they begin to sink; more fish than they ever saw before. What a sight that must have been! Life with Jesus will not be dull.

Peter is not amused and his reaction is interesting: *Go away from me, Lord, for I am a sinful man.* Simon already knows that Jesus is somehow a "holy man," but the kind of power he has just witnessed is too much for him. The contrast between Jesus and himself is terrifying. Simon does what many people do when confronted with God; rather than risk change, they try to get God to "go away." Jesus reassures Simon Peter with words that are said to the lowly many times in Luke, *Do not be afraid* (see also 1:13; 1:30; 2:10; 8:50). For those who put their trust in God, there is no need to be afraid of the power of God. For those who stand opposed to God, however, there is every reason to tremble.

Read **5:27-32**. Jesus' next call is to another "sinful man," sinful not by his own admission, but by society's judgment. Levi is a tax collector. He is therefore assumed to be a traitor and in all likelihood a thief. Jesus calls on him at his office. Jesus does not wait for people to come to worship to encounter God, but approaches them at work, in the midst of their daily chores, or on their sick beds. What made Levi drop everything? Luke records no miracle, no healing, no teaching associated with the call of Levi. We cannot know what experiences, if any, Levi had previously with Jesus. Jesus makes a demand on Levi, *Follow me,* and Levi obeys. As with the other three disciples, it costs him everything.

Read **6:12-16**. Here Luke records the names of Jesus' inner circle. Jesus chooses twelve men. This number is significant in Judaism. It is symbolic of the twelve tribes of Israel. These twelve are to receive a new designation, that of "apostle." The word "apostle" comes from the verb meaning "send out." Luke uses this title for the Twelve throughout his Gospel. The other Gospels rarely use it. In Luke's book of Acts the Twelve are sent out into the world with the gospel message.

In addition to the Twelve, throughout his ministry Jesus has crowds of disciples, both men and women. They have been set aside as those who will proclaim Jesus' message to all people. "Disciple" comes from a root meaning "learner." It is by far the most common word for Jesus' followers in the Gospels. See also Luke **8:19-21**. Here Jesus uses the phrase *those who hear the word of God and do it* to define his true family. His family is not the natural one but one composed of those who are faithful disciples and obedient to God.

Luke lists "Simon the Zealot" as one of the Twelve. "Zealot" could have a variety of meanings, but it usually denoted one who was a member of a group zealous about the Law. During the first century such groups provided strong resistance to Rome. They were often radical revolutionaries eager to take up arms against the oppressor.

Matthew's and Mark's lists of the apostles differ slightly from Luke's. John does not provide a list. Thaddeus is left out of Luke's list and replaced by a second Judas, *son of James*. Matthew's Gospel identifies Matthew as *the tax collector* (Matthew 10:3; see also Acts 1:13). Luke lists Matthew here (instead of the name "Levi") but does not designate him as the tax collector. Perhaps one or more of these men had two names (like Simon Peter/Cephas). Luke alone refers to Judas' betrayal with the rare and harsh word *traitor*.

Note once again Jesus' use of prayer. He prays all night before making this significant decision. This points up both the importance of prayer in Jesus' life and the important role these men will have in God's saving action.

## Women

Although the Twelve are men, women have a place among Jesus' inner circle. Read **8:1-3**. Luke tells us that several women at least occasionally accompanied Jesus and the apostles. These were all women who had been healed by Jesus. Luke names them: Mary Magdalene, Joanna, wife of Herod's steward, Susanna, *and many others who provided for them out of their resources*. Thus begins the long tradition in the church of the women's group being the only solvent organization!

Luke tells us that these women watched from a distance as Jesus was crucified (23:49). These are also the women who watched as Jesus' body was placed in the tomb (23:55-56) and who returned on Sunday morning to be the first witnesses (and preachers) of the resurrection (24:1).

## The Mission

Now read **9:1-6**. The role of the Twelve is specified in Jesus' instructions to the apostles at the beginning of their first mission. Jesus gives them the power to cure diseases and to cast out demons, then sends them out to proclaim the rule of God and to heal. In the ancient Middle East the custom of hospitality to strangers was important. One was expected to offer food and lodging to those on journeys. Jesus sends the disciples out, counting on the hospitality of the people to whom they will minister. The demand that they not take extra clothes or provisions will emphasize to the people that their visitors are dependent on God. They are not to stay in more than one house per town: *Whatever house you enter, stay there, and leave from there.* They must not insult the host by shopping around for nicer accommodations. The rabbis taught that even the dust of pagans was unclean. The gesture of shaking the dust off could mean that those who reject God's good news are not true Israelites.

Now we must look at some details of Jesus' ministry and particularly its focus on the kingdom of God. It will therefore be necessary to move about a bit in the chapters of the Gospel.

## *The Power of Jesus: Exorcism*

Jesus begins his work of healing in Capernaum. His healing miracles are signs of God's reign ("kingdom") beginning in the here and now. Many, but not all, healings come through the exorcism of a demon. Exorcism means the expelling of an evil spirit. There are no exorcisms in the Old Testament. They came into late Judaism through the Babylonian and Persian cultures. By Jesus' time they were accepted as rare, but possible; see **9:49-50**.

Five exorcisms, four of them healings, are recorded in detail during the Galilean phase of Jesus' ministry (chapters 4-9) although several others are alluded to (see 4:40-41, 6:18). These exorcisms have nothing in common with those in modern movies. Perhaps the most remarkable difference is that nowhere in the Bible do demons have any effect on a person's moral state. They cause some physical and psychological illnesses, but do not make the victim evil or demonic. People are not necessarily frightened of those who are possessed by demons; rather they are concerned about them. Evil spirits also do not necessarily cause mental aberrations. In another detailed description of an exorcism, **13:10-17**, the victim is only *bent over*.

Read **4:31-37**. In this story the demons know and acknowledge that Jesus is the Messiah. The title they use for him, *the Holy One of God*, is a messianic title. Perhaps Jesus refuses to allow the demons to speak because he does not want the crowds to misinterpret his mission. Perhaps it is because to call out a name gave one the power to curse that name.

It should be noted that Jesus, unlike non-Jews, uses no rituals, spells, incantations, or occult performances. He heals those with evil spirits by his word alone. He simply gives the order and the demons obey. The people are astonished that Jesus can dismiss demons with a word: *What kind of utterance is this?* (4:36). The Gerasene demoniac (8:29) and the father's boy (9:42) are also healed by Jesus' word alone. In 13:12 he heals a crippled woman by calling out, *Woman, you are free from your ailment*. He then touches her and she stands erect. There is no thought of any demons disobeying whatever Jesus commands. Those demoniacs that speak are reduced to begging (as in 8:28). Jesus' word is power. There is no question in Luke's Gospel of any evil power that is even remotely on a par with the power of God.

Because of these stories, the question often arises as to whether Jesus believed in demons. There is no sure way to know. He acted as though he believed in them. The physical illnesses and the mental despair that tormented the victims was real enough. But whether he considered demons as real or simply used the categories in which the people thought, Jesus destroyed sickness and anguish and put in their place health and wholeness.

Now read **4:38-41**. Luke includes here the healing of Simon's mother-in-law, although he has not yet introduced us to Simon (Peter). Jesus orders her fever to leave. The words *he … rebuked the fever* show that this, too, is an exorcism. Jesus heals many people as word spreads from neighbor to neighbor.

The story of the Gerasene demoniac in **8:26-39** is the longest and the oddest of the exorcisms. The man is possessed by multiple demons. Jesus demands the name for the purpose of the exorcism and is told that the demons' name is *Legion*. The abyss they mention was the prison of demons, but it was not beyond the reach of God's power.

The legion of demons begs Jesus to allow them to invade swine. Swine were unclean animals for Jews. They were kept only by Gentiles. Gerasa was a Gentile city. Jesus has, therefore, taken his ministry beyond the bounds of Israel to the Gentiles. This is, for Luke, an important event to include in his Gospel. Luke is concerned to show that God's grace is for the Gentile as well as the Jew. Remember that Luke's "Volume 2" (Acts) is a defense of the spread of Christianity beyond the borders of Israel.

The results of this exorcism on the local population are not positive. Like Peter, they ask Jesus to leave. Something far too powerful is here. It is disrupting the ordinary, which for them includes a demoniac, and it is costing them money–swine don't grow on trees! We will shortly see why the demons might have thought that they would be safe in the sea.

In **8:22-25** we have an exorcism that is not a healing. As far back as the book of Genesis large bodies of water signified chaos. In Genesis 1 God brings order out of the chaos of the deep, but when humanity sins, chaos reigns in the form of the flood. Bodies of water were the abodes of evil spirits. (Hence the legion of demons thought that they could escape into the sea.) The Jews for the most part were not fond of the sea and sailing. In the book of Revelation one of the great joys of the new creation is that *the sea was no more* (21:1).

Luke tells us Jesus *rebuked the wind and the raging waves*. This is the language of exorcism. It is not accurate to call this a "nature miracle." People of the New Testament did not deal with "nature" as an objective, scientifically controllable thing. All of creation was under God's control, including the demonic forces that invaded it.

What is most interesting about this event is that it is one of the few times when Jesus ministers to the disciples themselves. Yet Jesus seems amazed that he has to step in. *Where is your faith?* If there is one thing that can surprise Jesus it is the inability of people to trust God. He did not expect them to exorcise this "demon," for he had not yet given them that power. But, he is surprised that they were afraid. However, the fear generated by the storm is nothing compared to the fear and amazement they now feel concerning their master: *Who then is this, that he commands even the winds and the water, and they obey him?* That question is not answered here, and Jesus will shortly turn the tables and ask it of the disciples.

Read **9:37-43a**. Here is another case where Jesus is upset by the disciples' lack of faith. He is angered when the boy's father reports that the disciples could not cast out the spirit-demon. It is not clear why the disciples cannot perform the exorcism. They were given that power in 9:1-6. What is clear is that Jesus' power has not been diminished.

## *Other Healings*

Now Read **5:12-16**. There are several healing stories that are not exorcisms. Luke presents the healing of the leper as a typical case of this type. Leprosy could refer to any number of eruptive skin diseases. These ailments made a person ritually unclean. They engendered the kind of baseless fears that AIDS does in some quarters today. Read **Leviticus 13:45-46**. Not only did the leper violate the Law by approaching Jesus, but Jesus violated social conventions by touching the leper. Jesus shares the man's ostracism, but by sharing it destroys it. Unlike the healings by exorcism, the leper asks Jesus to heal him. He expresses unqualified faith, *Lord, if you choose, you can make me clean*. We will see that in many healings Jesus credits this kind of faith as the cause of the healing. (Note that here again Jesus instructs the man to fulfill the Jewish law).

Read **5: 17-26**. The healing of a paralytic immediately follows the cleansing of the leper and again demonstrates the power of faith to heal. It is not clear exactly whose faith is responsible: *When he saw their faith ...* This healing and the healing of the man with the withered hand (6:6-11) are recorded by Luke because they caused controversy with the religious authorities. We will deal more closely with these stories in the context of Jesus' conflicts with his enemies (Part 5).

Two more healings based on faith are included in Jesus' Galilean ministry. Read **7:1-10**. Here a Gentile comes to Jesus with a request for healing. It is interesting that the Jews deem this Gentile worthy of Jesus' help. Centurions were career men in the Roman army. The rank of centurion (commander of one-hundred foot soldiers) was the highest rank to which a regular army man could aspire. Centurions were very well paid and given a great deal of authority in the field.

Apparently this centurion is a God-fearer, one of the many Gentiles who worshiped the God of Israel but had not yet become Jewish converts. It is clear in this story that it is the faith of the person asking Jesus for help that is powerful, since the one being healed never appears in the story or is even heard from. The centurion's faith impresses Jesus, which is not an easy thing to do! Here again Jesus disregards the definition of God's people as only those who share the heritage of Israel. In fact, Jesus makes a point of it: *Not even in Israel have I found such faith.*

The centurion shows great respect for Jesus because he, too, as a soldier, understands having the authority to act. The centurion shows his deference by not even coming into Jesus' presence; he sends some Jewish elders to speak for him. He has complete faith that Jesus, as a commander, need only *speak the word*. Jesus heals the slave from a distance.

Read **8:43-48**. The healing of the woman with the hemorrhage is a second healing based on faith, using another means. The woman does not speak to Jesus at all, but surreptitiously touches him. Luke has mentioned before that power "came out" from Jesus when he was touched. Luke makes it sound almost like an electrical charge. It is Luke's way to put things in physical terms. But this is not magic. Jesus perceives the faith that leads the woman to touch him. He makes her healing public both to witness to the power of faith and to force the community to accept her as ritually clean again (see Leviticus 15:25-30).

The woman with the hemorrhage has interrupted Jesus' journey to heal a little girl who dies while Jesus is dealing with the woman. Read **8:40-42, 49-56**. Jesus tells the grieving father *Only believe*, have faith.

The raising of this girl is not the first instance of Jesus raising a person from the dead. Read **7:11-17**. The widow's son at Nain is raised, not because anyone asks Jesus to help, but purely because of Jesus' compassion for the mother. Without her only son, she would have no one to support her. It is difficult to explain why Jesus raises the widow's son in such a public way, and yet insists on secrecy when he heals the little girl (even going so far as to put off the paid mourners). At Nain the crowds labeled Jesus as a prophet. Perhaps Jesus' reasons for acting as he does have been obscured by Luke's arrangement of the contexts and chronology. Both of these raisings from the dead speak to the power of God at work in Jesus, before whom death simply crumbles.

## FOR FURTHER STUDY AND REFLECTION

### Memory Bank

Memorize the names of the apostles and of the women who accompanied Jesus.

### Research

1. Isaiah 42:1-4; 49:1-6; 50:4-9; and 52:13-53:12 are known as "Servant Songs." They deal with a suffering figure, and Jesus' ministry appears to have been strongly influenced by these passages. Review the "songs." In what ways can you identify their influence on Jesus?

2. Look up "zealot" in a Bible dictionary or other reference work. Why might a zealot, such as Simon, be attracted to Jesus?

### Reflection

1. What have you given up in order to be a disciple of Jesus? What might it be very difficult for you to give up?

2. Jesus' healings were signs of the presence of God's reign. What signs can you identify today as indications of the presence of that kingdom?

## SUMMARY

Jesus' ministry of teaching and healing arouses controversy with the religious authorities. The conflicts center on who can forgive sins, Jesus' practice of socializing with sinners and tax collectors, when to fast, and what it means to observe the Sabbath. Jesus' answers to his critics make them determined that something drastic must be done about him.

The ministry in Galilee culminates in the feeding of the 5000, which is reminiscent of God's feeding of the Israelites in the wilderness. It also looks ahead to the eucharistic meal and speaks volumes about the mission of Christ's church.

Immediately following Peter's declaration that Jesus is the Messiah, Jesus begins to speak about his impending death. The journey to Jerusalem, where Jesus will do battle with the final foe, is about to begin.

## BASIC BIBLE REFERENCES

Luke 5:17-39
    6:1-11
    9:7-36 43b-48
    11:37-44
    20:45-47
Exodus 20:8-11; 23:12
Deuteronomy 5:12-15

## WORD LIST

halachah
Pharisee
scribe
sinner
sabbath
theophany
shechinah

# Ministry in Galilee Continues

## *Pharisees and Scribes*

The popularity of Jesus' ministry draws attention not only from the common people, but from the religious and political authorities as well. Luke tells the reader that Pharisees and teachers of the Law *had come from every village of Galilee and Judea and Jerusalem* (5:17) to listen to his teaching. These teachers of the Law (scribes) and Pharisees will become Jesus' chief antagonists, although some will secretly become disciples.

Who were these people? The teachers of the Law were professionals concerned with the Law of Moses, the Torah. In the Israel of Jesus' day there was no separate civil law. The Torah and the interpretations of it served as both religious and civil law. These scribes had two functions: 1) to teach the Law to all Israel, and 2) to interpret the Law. The task of interpretation meant, for the most part, handing down the traditional legal judgments, known among Jews as "halachah." The scribes were less concerned with teaching the simple meaning of the texts and more concerned with preserving the traditional legal system that had been founded on the texts. As those who preserved God's law and the traditional legal judgments concerning it, the scribes were honored and respected. However, for many of them this honor and respect seem to have inflated their egos to dangerous proportions. Read Jesus' strong comments on this in **20:45-47**. Scribes could belong to any of the current religious-political parties, such as the Pharisees or Sadducees. Often the scribes in question are referred to as the "scribes of the Pharisees."

The Pharisees, in contrast to the scribes, were laymen. The Pharisees interpreted the Law of the Hebrew Scriptures in terms of its proper contemporary observance and with reference to the traditions. They were strict in the accuracy of their interpretations and in their scrupulous observance of the Law. It was their willingness to back up their interpretations of the Law with the way they lived that gained them wide respect. At the time of Jesus they were a very influential group within Judaism.

The Pharisees' strict legalism led to an insistence on careful attention to ritual purification. It also accounted for their determination to remain separate from the common people. Such people had neither the means nor the opportunity to observe carefully all the rituals and laws that had been passed down and which the Pharisees insisted were necessary. This "tradition of the elders" is what separated the Pharisees from the Sadducees, who were more literalistic and rejected traditions not contained in the Torah itself. Some Pharisees became disciples of Jesus, including Joseph of Arimathea (23:50), Nicodemus (John 3:1) and later Paul (Philippians 3:5b).

The role of the scribes and Pharisees in attempting to preserve Judaism in the face of attempts by the Greek and Roman empires to eradicate all other cultures and religions should not be forgotten. An oppressed people needs to keep its identity and remember its basic precepts if it is to survive. It was not this role of the Pharisees in Judaism that finally caused their break with Jesus. It was the desire on the part of many of them to preserve the status quo, both for political reasons and in order to maintain their positions of authority. This led them into terrible hypocrisy. Again Jesus makes harsh comments: read **11:37- 44**.[1]

## *The Conflicts Begin*

Read **5:17-26** again. We first meet the scribes and Pharisees here. Luke does not suggest that they have come with any particular axe to grind, but have probably come to hear for themselves whether this popular preacher and healer is in line with Jewish orthodoxy. It is no surprise that when Jesus says, *Friend, your sins are forgiven you*, they begin to ask questions. According to both the Old Testament and the rabbinical tradition only God can forgive sins. Jesus has no credentials to allow him to exercise the right of absolution. They ask, *Who is this who is speaking blasphemies? Who can forgive sins but God alone?*

Jesus' answer implies that the authority to forgive sins is given by the same God who gives the authority to heal. After all, even the crowds have recognized that it is God's power at work in Jesus' acts of healing (see Luke 7:16). In order to show his authority to forgive sins, which has no observable signs, Jesus demonstrates his authority to heal, a power with

---

1  We will discuss these verses again in Part 8.

clearly observable signs. Luke does not record any negative impact on the part of the Pharisees and scribes. He simply says, *Amazement seized all of them, and they glorified God ...*

## Table Manners

The call of Levi provides another opportunity for the Pharisees and their scribes to confront Jesus. Read **5:27-32** again. This time they will challenge him on the grounds that he does not keep the religious traditions. *Why do you eat and drink with tax collectors and sinners?* We have already looked at the particular sins of tax collectors (see Part 3). To call someone a sinner was not simply a personal opinion of another's moral state. Sinner was a technical term for someone whose breach of the Law of Moses was public knowledge. It may have been formally noted. The sinner was, therefore, excluded from the local synagogue, making him an outcast in the community.

In this story Jesus, whom the Pharisees and scribes view as an insider–an observant son of Israel–is including the excluded. The Pharisees were careful in the extreme to exclude those who did not keep the Law; Jesus seems to be carelessly including the outsiders. Jesus makes it clear that it is not carelessness on his part: *I have come to call not the righteous but sinners to repentance.* Jesus leaves it for his hearers to decide whether they are well or sick.

In Judaism, as in cultures all over the world today, to eat with someone is an expression of friendship and equality. Jesus not only eats with tax collectors and sinners, he allows them to throw a party in his honor. Only your friends throw you a party. Table fellowship and Sabbath observance are two of the marks of the observant Jew that the Pharisees are most concerned about as they seek to hold Judaism together. Jesus' inclusion of outsiders at the table undermines the Pharisees' practice of eating only with the ritually pure.

In their accounts of this story neither Matthew (9:13) nor Mark (2:17) includes the words *to repentance.* Luke uses the word repentance more than all the other New Testament writers together. He means to emphasize that the gospel has ethical implications; acceptance demands change.

The Pharisees and scribes are not finished yet with their criticisms of Jesus. They have more questions about his "table manners." Read **5:33-39**. Pharisees fasted twice a week, Mondays and Thursdays. Fasting was one of the three good works of Judaism, the others being prayer and giving alms. Both the disciples of the Pharisees and the disciples of John the Baptizer fasted frequently. Jesus' disciples did not. Jesus answers that fasting at this time is inappropriate. He interprets fasting as a form of grieving for one's sins. But how can one fast when God is in the very act of forgiving those sins? It's time to party, and that is just what

Jesus and his disciples are doing. The first inklings of the cross, however, are here (note 5:35). Fasting will then be the right thing to do.

Whether the parables of the garment and the wineskins, which are attached to this section, originally occurred in this context is difficult to say. Verse 39, in fact, does not seem to fit with the rest. This is the first parable that Luke presents. We will reserve full discussion on parables until Part 7. This parable, addressed to Jesus' detractors, implies that what Jesus is doing is something new and cannot be sewn on like a patch to the old ways which the Pharisees hold so dear. The excitement of the new life will split the frail skins of the old traditions.

## *Sabbath Stories*

Luke immediately sets before the reader two more controversy stories. Read **6:1-11**. Both deal with keeping the sabbath. "Sabbath" referred to the seventh day of the week, sundown Friday until sundown Saturday. There were also other holy days set aside as "sabbaths." In Jesus' day sabbath observance had become one of the most important reminders to God's people that they were set apart from the pagans who surrounded and ruled them. The sabbath laws expressly state that no work was to be done on the sabbath; read **Exodus 20:8-11; 23:12, Deuteronomy 5:12-15**. This left much room for questions. What constituted work? Obviously some things had to be done. The Pharisees and scribes were the ones who answered these practical questions.

The extremes to which the Pharisees were willing to go in interpreting the sabbath law is illustrated by their first complaint against Jesus' disciples. Plucking the grain was perfectly legal. The complaint was that when the disciples rubbed the heads of grain between their hands to remove the chaff, they were threshing. This violated the law against working on the sabbath. Jesus counters their argument with a similar situation from 1 Samuel 21:1-6. He then declares himself to be *lord of the sabbath*. Jesus, not the Pharisees nor the scribes, defines what is appropriate sabbath observance. The one who has authority to forgive sins and to heal also has authority over the laws and traditions of Israel.

The next incident does not immediately follow the first. Luke puts these stories together as examples of Jesus' teaching about the sabbath. Note the vague introductions to each story. On this occasion Jesus is teaching in a synagogue in the presence of scribes and Pharisees. But here Jesus' detractors have become his enemies. They are watching for an opportunity to accuse him of wrongdoing. Often in Luke's Gospel Jesus is portrayed as knowing intuitively what others are thinking. This is the case in 6:8. Jesus, in defiance of their unspoken threat, phrases his question to them in such a way that to do nothing on the sabbath is not an option. He then heals the man without touch, words, or even prayer.

Note how these particular scribes and Pharisees reveal what is truly in their hearts. There is no joy in them for the man who has been healed. They could not care less about him. It is Jesus' refusal to accept their interpretation of the Sabbath commands that infuriates them. He is not yielding to their authority. They hold their first meeting to consider *what they might do to Jesus*. Healing on the Sabbath is, according to them, a sin, while plotting mayhem on the Sabbath apparently is not. They have completely forgotten the spirit of God's Law. It is a matter now of slavish legalism and a fight to hold on to their authority.

## Another Enemy

Now read **9:7-9**. Here is another enemy and Jesus will be confronted with his authority as well. He is Herod Antipas, son of Herod the great and tetrarch of Galilee. It is this Herod who had John killed. It is therefore not simply curiosity that made him want to see Jesus. Herod is anxious about anyone who is generating great crowds. The last thing Herod needs is a popular uprising. Note that Herod and Jesus' disciples (9:18) have heard the same rumors about Jesus' identity. We will look at those rumors shortly. Herod's shadow will continue to loom. He reappears in 13:31 desiring to kill Jesus and in 23:6-12, when Herod finally meets Jesus and tries unsuccessfully to interrogate him.

## Feeding the 5000

The feeding of the 5000 is one of the few events told in all four Gospels. Read **9:10-17**. Only Luke locates it in a wilderness region outside Bethsaida. Bethsaida, according to John's Gospel, is the hometown of Peter, Andrew, and Philip (John 1:44). The crowd was not expected. Jesus had taken the apostles away for a retreat and a debriefing after their return from their mission of preaching and healing (Luke 9:1-6). It is Jesus' habit to get away for prayer, for renewal (Mark 6:31), and to clear his head after times of praise or success. He may be attempting to instill those same habits in his inner circle. Luke's readers are not given the apostles' full report (9:10). The crowds, having found out where Jesus has gone, interrupt his retreat. Note, however, that Jesus is not upset about the interruption (9:11b). These are the people for whom he came and he lavishes the news of the kingdom and healing on them.

The disciples' concern for the crowds is met by Jesus' challenge to the disciples to care for the people: *You give them something to eat.* The disciples meet that challenge with the complaint that they have insufficient resources. Jesus' insight into the ways people function is noted in his directions to the disciples. The people are organized into manageable groups and made to sit down. Seated people cannot surge forward. People in small groups are not part of a mob.

Were the loaves and fishes physically multiplied, or did the people, shamed by Jesus' willingness to give away all the food he had, begin to bring out and share what they had brought into the wilderness with them? Either might be seen as a miracle. Luke is not interested in how the miracle happened.

Jesus blesses the food and the disciples distribute it. What should be noted here is the way in which Jesus' actions are described: *taking … blessed … broke … gave.* These are the words used to describe Jesus' actions at the Lord's Supper. By the time of the writing of this Gospel these words were already familiar in the liturgy of the church. Jesus' love and compassion for those in need foreshadows the Eucharist. Luke immediately follows this story with Peter's confession and Jesus' first mention of his impending death. The feeding of the 5000, table fellowship with all who would come, giving all for others, precede the announcement of death.

As is so often the case in Luke's Gospel, there are echoes of Old Testament stories. The feeding of the multitude by miraculous means in a *deserted place* reminds the reader of God's care for the Hebrew people in their wanderings in the desert after the exodus from Egypt. The God of the Exodus is at work in Jesus of Nazareth.

## *The Turning Point*

The Pharisees have asked *Who is this?* (5:21b). The disciples have asked *Who is this?* (8:25). Herod has asked *Who is this?* (9:9). Read **9:18-20**. It is Jesus' turn to ask, and he demands an answer. His first question *Who do the crowds say that I am?* is met with three replies: 1) *John the Baptizer;* 2) *Elijah;* 3) *one of the ancient prophets.* All three answers are in terms of prophets. The crowds accept John as a prophet sent by God (20:6), and John's father prophesies through the Holy Spirit: *and you, child, will be called the prophet of the Most High; for you will go before the Lord to prepare his ways* (1:76). Elijah was the prophet designated in the Old Testament and the traditional Jewish writings as the forerunner of the *day of the Lord,* the end time (Malachi 4:5). Others apparently saw in Jesus the authoritative teachings that had marked the great prophets of old, teachings that had been warnings that the crisis time was upon the people, the time to decide for or against God's Will. Jesus, then, was seen as a prophet in the style of the prophets of old or as the forerunner to the Messiah who inaugurates the new age.

From the opening chapter of his work Luke has interwoven the question of Jesus' identity with a myriad of ways of answering that question. The prophecies of the first two chapters clearly explain who this Jesus is to be. In the baptism of Jesus God gives the answer (3:22b). The temptation of Jesus reminds us that Jesus must freely choose to be what God has sent him to be. His acceptance of his role is announced at Nazareth (4:18-22) and boldly proclaimed by a host of power-filled acts and authoritative teaching. He is the one who heals mental and physical illness, sets down the terms of religious observance, brings life to the dead, forgives sins, and feeds God's people. The crowd's belief that Jesus is a prophet or the forerunner of the Messiah is far too low an estimation. The question must be asked once more: *But who do you say that I am?*

The fact that Luke introduces this episode by telling us that Jesus was at prayer immediately before asking the question of his identity lets us know that this conversation will be a significant one. Peter's answer, *The Messiah of God,* repudiates the three previous answers. Jesus is no mere prophet, no forerunner of Messiah. He himself is Messiah. The phrase *of God* reminds us that the center of this story, the one who acts, is God.

## *Jesus Speaks of Death and Resurrection*

Read **9:21-22**. Jesus demands silence, then immediately begins to reinterpret for the disciples just what this messiahship will mean. It is nothing like the popular concept of Messiah as the one who would rescue Israel from political oppression. There is no parallel in the Old Testament or in Jewish tradition for Jesus' description of Messiah: *The Son of Man must undergo great suffering, and be rejected by the elders, chief priests, and scribes, and be killed, and on the third day be raised.* The passages in Isaiah about the suffering servant are not a description of the Messiah. Jesus combines the suffering of God's servant with the ushering in of the kingdom, which is the role of the Messiah. Nothing could have prepared Jesus' disciples for this new definition of Messiah. A dramatic confirmation of the correctness of Peter's declaration will come very shortly in the transfiguration.

Some believe the prediction of the resurrection on the lips of Jesus in 9:22 was added by the early church in order to show Jesus' complete knowledge. Jesus predicts his death three times in the Gospel. See 9:21-22; **9:43b-45**; 18:31-34. Twice he includes details of his torture as well as foretelling the resurrection. In two passages the disciples are totally confused; they simply cannot accept what they are hearing.

## *The Cost of Discipleship*

Given this new definition of Messiah, what must then be the role of Messiah's disciples? Read **9:23-27**. Here is the call for disciples to *take up their cross daily.* Taking up the cross is a conscious choice. It is not some loathsome burden imposed by "fate." Jesus' followers must intentionally lay aside everything that gets in the way of obedient discipleship. The words "every day" make this demand an ethical one rather than a call to martyrdom. *Follow me* means to copy Jesus' life in one's own life, to follow in his path. This, too, is the pattern of every day. To save one's life has the sense of preserving or protecting one's life. Not getting involved in life might be mistaken for saving one's life, but in reality one is not living at all. Losing one's life need not refer to a martyr's death, but to the giving, the spending of one's life for others in obedience to God's will.

The final sentence of the passage speaks of seeing the kingdom. For Luke, and for Jesus, the kingdom of God was present in the person of Jesus and could be entered now by trusting in him. It was also future, to be consummated by God at the close of history.

## *The Transfiguration*

The disciples could hardly be expected to understand and accept this definition of messiahship. Their lack of perception is clearly evident in the argument among them reported in **9:46-48**. They need to come to grips with what is about to happen to Jesus and what their role is to be. According to Luke, Jesus takes the inner circle up onto a mountain to pray, and there they receive confirmation of all that Jesus has told them. It is significant that this confirmation comes shortly after Jesus' first prediction of his passion.

Continue on to read **9:28-36**. The fact that Jesus is praying assures us of the importance of the following scene. In Matthew 17:9 Jesus describes these events as a vision. Luke does not explain what the event is. It is, however, parallel to Jesus' baptism; it is another "theophany," a showing forth of God. At Jesus' baptism the descent of the Holy Spirit, God's presence, came in the form of a dove. The voice of God confirmed Jesus as God's Son. Here on the mountain God's presence is made known by the cloud, known in the Hebrew Scriptures as the "Shechinah" (see Exodus 13:21; 24:15-18; 40:34). Again God speaks, using virtually the same words in 9:35 as we read earlier in 3:22b.

This time the voice is for the benefit of the three disciples. This reconfirmation that Jesus is God's Son affirms that what Jesus has said about his suffering and death is, indeed, the path that God approves. He is still the Messiah. The presence of Elijah and Moses adds to the confirmation. Elijah is a prophet and forerunner of the Messiah. Moses is the lawgiver. Together they represent "the Law and the Prophets," a term used by Jesus for the Scriptures (16:29). Only Luke gives us the content of the conversation they hold with Jesus. In 9:31 they speak of Jesus' impending *departure* (the Greek word is *exodos*). The Law and the Prophets, therefore, also testify to the death, resurrection, and ascension of the Messiah. Jesus' path of suffering and self-sacrifice is confirmed by the Scriptures and by God.

## FOR FURTHER STUDY AND REFLECTION

### Memory Bank

1. Study the differences among the Pharisees, Sadducees, and scribes so you can describe these groups to another person.

### Research

1. In a Bible dictionary or other reference volume, read about the doctrines and beliefs of the Pharisees. What did they hold in common with Jesus? What positive role did they play in their nation in Jesus' time?

2. Research the importance of sabbath observance in the first century. Why did it become one of the most important of all Jewish rituals?

### Reflection

1. Luke presents Jesus as the Son of God, who has authority over everything. Some persons are satisfied to see him as a moral teacher, as someone less than the Messiah. Who do you say that Jesus is? On what do you base your belief?

2. Try writing a statement of faith to express your understanding of Jesus.

3. When have you been tempted to side with the Pharisees and scribes against the demands of Jesus? How have you coped with the temptation?

## SUMMARY

Luke presents a block of Jesus' teaching in the form of a discourse given on *a level place*. This is a shorter version of what is known in Matthew as the Sermon on the Mount. The "sermon" has five themes: blessings and woes, love of enemies, judging, integrity, hearing and doing. Other teachings that Luke places within the Galilean ministry are the parables of the Two Debtors, The Sower and its interpretation, the Lamp Under a Jar, and the Two Builders.

## BASIC BIBLE REFERENCES

Luke 6:17-49
     7:36-50
     8:4-18

## WORD LIST

parable
beatitude
blessing
hyperbole
allegory
eschaton

*6*

# Ministry in Galilee: Teaching

## The Teachings on the Plain

Begin by reading **6:17-19**. This begins the section of Luke sometimes referred to as the Sermon on the Plain (NRSV and NIV, *a level place*). It contains some of the material also found in Matthew's Sermon on the Mount (Matthew 5, 6, and 7), but Luke's version is only one-fourth as long. Luke includes much of Matthew's material later on. None of this material is found in Mark or John. In both Matthew and Luke the sermon, as we refer to it, follows the call of the disciples and concludes with the parable of the Two Builders.

## The Audience

Three separate groups of people are present: the apostles (*them,*) *a great crowd of his disciples,* and *a great multitude.* The crowd comes from Judea, including Jerusalem in the south and Tyre and Sidon in the north. Those from the north may well include Gentiles. They come not only to listen but to be healed.

It is the disciples who are addressed in the sermon itself (verse 20a). The words that follow apply to those who have chosen to follow Jesus. The admonitions to a particular way of life, therefore, are not advice for the crowds, but statements of the way life is in the kingdom community.

Look at 7:1. Although Jesus' teaching was addressed specifically to the disciples, it was done publicly so that the crowds mentioned in chapter 6 heard everything that Jesus said. They have been introduced to what it would mean for them to become disciples. Nowhere does Luke give any indication that there was any formal recognition of discipleship beyond Jesus' choosing of the Twelve and sending out of the seventy. Apparently anyone who put faith in Jesus and resolved to live in obedience to God's love could be considered a follower.

The sermon in Luke is limited to five themes: blessings and woes, love for enemies, judging, integrity, and hearing and doing. We will look at each of these in turn.

## *Blessings and Woes*

Read **6:20-26**. A beatitude is a literary form that begins with the word "blessed" or "happy." The word used here for "blessed" in the Greek describes the highest form of happiness. It has the force of "congratulations."

Since the intended audience has been identified as the disciples, it seems strange that the woes are also included here. It may be that Luke has included this negative list to show the contrast between those who are blessed and those who are condemned. Perhaps this passage recalls another incident where both blessings and woes were announced to God's people Israel; see Deuteronomy 11:26-28.

In pronouncing these blessings Jesus defines what is blessed. He does not offer references from the Scriptures to back up what he says. The definitions of the blessed are his own. It is because Jesus says that the poor, the hungry, the weeping, and the rejected are blessed that it is so. Here the power of Jesus' word defines reality.

Why are they blessed? It is because the reign of God turns upside down human categories so that the poor become rich, the hungry filled, the sorrowful joyful, and the rejected accepted. This reversal of fortune has been a theme since the beginning of the gospel: *He has brought down the powerful from their thrones, and lifted up the lowly; he has filled the hungry with good things, and sent the rich away empty* (1:52-53). The blessings, like Mary's song, look forward to that eschatological day when God's reign will be complete.

But do these sayings apply only to the end of time, when the kingdom comes in all its fullness? In 6:21 and 25 Jesus contrasts the way things are now and the way they will be, which indicates that this blessedness is indeed for the time to come. Note, however, 6:20b: *Blessed are you who are poor, for yours is the kingdom of God.* The fulfillment of the kingdom is future, but in Jesus the reign of God is breaking into human society even now. *Today this scripture has been fulfilled,* Jesus declared in the synagogue at Nazareth (4:21). The future is completely assured; sorrow and suffering are being changed into victory and joy even now. Again, the church's agenda is set: it is the poor, the hungry, the sorrowing and those who are suffering for the faith that have claim on the church's attention. Luke does not spiritualize the poor and the hungry. He understands Jesus to mean the financially poor and the physically hungry.

The woes can be interpreted along the same lines. In 6:26 Jesus offers a warning that to be honored and admired by the world may mean that you have been co-opted by this world and are completely out of touch with God's will. For Jesus, our lives are always tied to the lives of God's suffering children. To be content with wealth while others starve is the only contentment the rich will know; to those who laugh in the face of another's misery, the reversals in the kingdom will bring an end to their laughter. Our relationship to God can be read in the relationships we have with others.

## *Love for Enemies*

Move on to **6:27-36**. This section is composed of two parts, instruction (verses 27-31) and explanation (verses 32-36). In the first part Jesus makes it clear that his followers are to act in precisely the opposite way from what the world expects. They are not to copy the ways of their enemies. The hated does not hate, the cursed does not curse, the abused does not abuse, the one hit does not strike. These instructions are not suggestions, they are commands. One set under authority obeys commands because they are commands, not because one necessarily feels like obeying. Theologian Paul Tillich once said, "In Christianity the truth is found if it is done." In following the commands we discover the truth inherent in them. We do not wait until we agree with Jesus; we obey, and in obeying we discover that his word is truth.

The instruction section ends with what is usually called the Golden Rule. This injunction is found in many writings previous to the time of Jesus but almost always in negative form. Jesus moves the idea past that of doing no wrong (which a dead man could fulfill) to the positive actions of love. Life in the kingdom is not one of merely keeping oneself unstained from evil. It is a life that produces love and community.

The explanation for these orders is that if the victims were to react in kind, they would be renouncing God's reign over their lives. They would be bowing down to the power of evil. As soon as a person retaliates with hatred and violence, evil has gained another subject. "Evil propagates by contagion. It can be contained and defeated only when hatred, insult, and injury are absorbed and neutralized by love"[1]. The actions of others do not dictate to Jesus' followers. His disciples do not react to what others do; rather they act out of their allegiance to God. Discipleship, not provocation, defines the response. A response that is independent of the actions of others is a mature response. Disciples are to love, regardless of the situation.

This in no way is to suggest that anyone who is being abused, physically, mentally, or spiritually, should just sit and "take it." Jesus enjoins his followers to pray for those who abuse them, but he does not insist that they remain in a situation that invites abuse. To "turn the other cheek" is an immediate response to violence against one's person; it is not dictated as a way of life. The original context of turning the other cheek may have been a situation where one is struck because one is a Christian. The prayers for the abuser may have to be said from afar. It is illegitimate to pervert these sayings in order to perpetuate actions which are clearly against the spirit of Jesus' love. It is hardly in the realm of loving one's neighbor to allow that neighbor to continue to sin.

Those who think that these sayings are for a simpler time and place need only remember that the people to whom Jesus spoke were living in enemy-occupied territory where provocations were not uncommon. Roman soldiers could force civilians to carry their packs for a mile (Matthew 5:41). Extortion by soldiers and threats of violence were not uncommon. Jesus' followers, however, take their orders not from their emotions, their anger, or their egos, but from God. The children of God are those whose actions imitate God's: ... *you will be children of the Most High; for he is kind to the ungrateful and the wicked.* ... Matthew's parallel to Luke's *Be merciful, just as your Father is merciful* has led many to throw their hands up in dismay, for Matthew reads, *Be perfect, therefore, as your heavenly Father is perfect* (5:48). In most people's minds the word "perfect" means completely without flaws or faults, never making a mistake. This is a rather unfortunate translation of a word that can mean perfect, but also means "complete," "full-grown," "mature." Luke uses a different word which means "compassionate" or "merciful." Both Gospels call followers to a mature, God-centered response to others.

## *Passing Judgment*

Now read **6:37-38**. These commands are concerned with judging, condemning, forgiving, and giving. The opposite of judging and condemning is not having no opinion, but forgiving. It would not be possible to forgive a wrong if one did not recognize that a wrong had been done. The disciple is instructed to give, to make the first move. What is given is mercy, compassion, forgiveness. Jesus makes it clear that the way we act toward others is

---

1   George B. Caird, *The Gospel of St. Luke* (Baltimore: Penguin Books, 1963) p. 104.

the way God acts toward us; God's mercy is tied to our mercy. (The petition for forgiveness in the Lord's Prayer (11:4) is another reminder that God ties our plea for mercy to our forgiving of others.)

The word translated *lap* in 6:38 originally meant a huge pocket formed by pulling the robe out above the belt, something like carrying grain in an apron. What we gain from our obedience to these commands is mercy and forgiveness in wonderful abundance, *a good measure, pressed down, shaken together, running over.* The reward of obedience is forgiveness and joy.

Read **6:39-42**. Perhaps this section was not originally connected with the preceding verses. The idea that joins the two sections is that of passing judgment. Jesus was fond of using "hyperbole," that is, using outlandish statements in order to make a point. *Why do you see the speck in your neighbor's eye, but do not notice the log in your own eye?* That anyone could fail to notice a log in the eye is outrageous to the point of being humorous. Jesus' message is clear: human beings have far too much work to do on their own sins and shortcomings without presuming to have time to cure their neighbors. The word *hypocrite* is taken from the theater. There it meant an actor, one who wore a mask. There can be no followers of Jesus who are play-acting. They cannot be persons who lead but cannot see, who teach what they have not learned, who heal others when they themselves need healing first.

## Integrity

Read **6:43-45**. In the thinking of Jesus' day the heart was the seat of the intellect, not of the emotions. The good fruit brought forth from a sound mind will be good counsel and wise action based on clear-sightedness, intelligent thinking, and self-knowledge. Our speech reveals our true nature. In Luke and in Acts the presence of the Holy Spirit is shown when a person speaks. A person can only speak words of mercy, forgiveness, and counsel if the mind is full of these same qualities. In order to have integrity, what a person does, says, and thinks must be one.

## The Two Builders

If one's word is the focus of the preceding verses, then **6:46-49** provides a correction. There will always be those who by their insincere words try to hide what is in their hearts. They are "all talk." They do not believe with heart or mind what they say. They do not act on the words coming out of their mouths. *Why do you call me 'Lord, Lord' and do not do what I tell you?* A person is your Lord if his word is authoritative for you; if you do as he says. The one who speaks of Jesus as Lord without the actions to substantiate those words is trying to build his life on a lie. He has no inner integrity; words and actions do not match.

Such a person, therefore, has a very wobbly foundation on which to build a life. The one who not only hears and mouths the words of Jesus but who also does what Jesus commands is building a life of integrity on a solid foundation. This integrity or the lack of it may not be obvious in the day-to-day course of living. But when the difficult times come, the integrity of the foundation will become obvious. These words must have carried special meaning for early Christians who put themselves in danger when they publicly proclaimed that *Jesus is Lord.*

## A Sinful Woman

Skip over to **7:36-50**. Jesus was frequently a dinner guest of Pharisees. He did not refuse table fellowship with anyone, either the sinners who knew they were sinners or the sinners who thought they were righteous. We cannot know Simon's motives, but there are clues as to what he thought of Jesus. He does not greet Jesus in the customary ways of friendship and hospitality. It is possible that Simon has invited Jesus in order to see whether he really is a prophet. He is, therefore, wary of Jesus, waiting until Jesus proves himself before offering him friendship.

The unnamed woman is most likely a prostitute. We have before us two religious men and a sinner. Simon's understanding of right behavior in this situation is to judge her and avoid contact. Jesus accepts her acts of gratitude and love and blesses her.

The parable of the Two Debtors, which Jesus puts before Simon, makes use of a theme common in Jesus' parables: an unpayable debt. Both debtors are unable to pay. Simon does not realize the situation he is in; he does not see himself as a debtor to God. The woman obviously sees clearly her position before God. She has responded to Jesus' message of forgiveness; Simon does not think it applies to him. The woman's acceptance of God's forgiveness issues in loving actions done out of gratitude. Simon's actions are ungracious and his thoughts judgmental.

In this incident we see how two religious men react to a sinner. But Jesus turns the event so that what becomes important is how Simon and the woman react to him. The dinner guests are offended by Jesus' pronouncement of forgiveness since only God can forgive sins. Jesus' blessing of the woman is typical of his response to those who are healed (saved). We will see it again many times. We may note in passing that this story of a sinful woman is contrasted with the passage describing women disciples, which immediately follows in 8:1-3.

## *Parables²*

Matthew, Mark, and Luke all agree that teaching by parables was Jesus' favorite form of instruction. (There are no parables as such in John.) Mark writes, *he did not speak to them except in parables ...* (4:34a). The rabbis had for a long time used parables extensively in their teaching. In fact, parables go back well into the Old Testament. We shall see in succeeding sessions that Jesus, on occasion, reworked old, familiar parables, giving them surprise endings.

Jesus' parables come in several forms. They can be brief figurative sayings, such as the blind leading the blind (Luke 6:39), similitudes (or pictures), such as the fig tree as a harbinger of summer, or full-blown stories. Similitudes use a general truth (a south wind brings heat), while the full parable tells a story about a particular individual or type of individual: *A certain creditor had two debtors.* Parables, then, range from the simple to the complex. Generally speaking, figurative sayings have one verb, the similitudes two or more verbs, and parables have a series of verbs which are in the past tense. C.H. Dodd has given an insightful definition of a parable: "At its simplest, the parable is a metaphor or simile drawn from nature or common life, arresting the hearer by its vividness or strangeness, and leaving the mind in sufficient doubt about its precise application to tease it into active thought."³

Parables can sound deceptively simple, for they speak about simple things: household chores, daily work, farming, family, nature, and the like. But the real subjects of parables are the crucial truths of life. Instead of telling us what to think, Jesus uses parables to make us think.

A word needs to be said about "allegory." In an allegorical story *everything* is symbolic. In the parable of the Lost Sons (Luke 15:11-32) the father and each son are symbolic, but the details are not. They are simply the details of any true-to-life story. But in an allegory everything tends to be symbolic. Beginning in the third century some church theologians took Jesus' parables and turned them into fantastic allegories. It is important to be very wary of giving symbolic meaning to the details of a parable. We should ask ourselves one simple question when we deal with sayings of Jesus: What would Jesus' first hearers have understood? This helps us to avoid reading into Jesus' teachings ideas that were not originally there. Occasionally, however, allegorical detail does appear, as we shall shortly see.

---

2   The bulk of Jesus' sayings and parables are reserved by Luke for the journey to Jerusalem (Parts 7-10) and the ministry in Jerusalem (Part 11).

3   C. H. Dodd, *The Parables of the Kingdom* (New York: Scribners, 1961) p. 16.

## The Story of the Sower and Its Interpretation

Now read **8:4-15**. Here is a full-scale parable and an interpretation if it. We will look at the parts separately. Luke does not give any particular occasion for this parable. It is told to a *great crowd* gathered from many towns.

Because parables, by their nature, deal with the common stuff of every day, we need to become familiar with some of the details of life in first-century Palestine. Would the first hearers of this story have found anything strange or unusual about it? Probably not. A farmer went about his business of broadcasting seed (flinging it by handfuls from a sack at his side). Some of the seed is unproductive, for a variety of reasons all of which are common enough, but some seed produces in unusual abundance. To the Palestinian there would have been nothing strange about the seed being sown onto a hard path, or into the weeds, or onto rocks. The people knew that Palestinian farmers sowed the seed first and then plowed the ground. To plow first in that very dry climate would have allowed the ground's moisture to evaporate before the seeds were in the earth.

The disciples, at least, know that because Jesus is Jesus, this story must have a deeper meaning than at first appears. Jesus' reply to their question (verses 9-10) seems to be confusing. His rather free rendering of Isaiah 6:9 sounds as if he does not want *others* to understand. But *others* do not see the kingdom in the words of Jesus because they do not see the kingdom at work in Jesus. It matters a great deal that it is Jesus who speaks. For the unbelieving crowds, it is only the superficial words that matter. If they knew Jesus, they would look more deeply into the parable as, in fact, the disciples are doing.

The interpretation of the parable is allegorical. In the explanation the seed is the Word of God, the seeds on the path are those lured away by the devil, the ones on the rock are shallow people who fail during persecution, the ones in the thorns are those choked off by the interests of the world. It is only the seeds in the good soil which bear fruit with patience.

The early church needed this interpretation in order to speak to the needs of its struggling communities. Early Christians found themselves in very trying circumstances. The gospel at its beginning made little headway; the church was not large, and moreover it was beginning to feel persecution (*a time of testing*). They must have wondered if their witnessing and work would ever produce fruit. This interpretation of the parable of The Sower encourages the church not to give up, even though the situation looks pathetic and the rewards, so far, meager. The message for them is in verse 15: *But as for that in the good soil, these are the ones who, when they hear the word, hold it fast in an honest and good heart, and bear fruit with patient endurance.* The call was to hold fast, not to give up in the face of adversity–a message we need to hear.

The primary point of The Sower is that although the kingdom does not look as though it is making much headway, the final result (the eschaton) will be marvelous. Tiny beginnings belie the fullness of the outcome. The random circumstances of the seeds would not at first have had the importance that they came to have in the interpretation. But the essential point is the same. Do not be dismayed by small beginnings, for the glorious consummation is assured.

## *A Lamp Under a Jar*

Finally, read **8:16-18**. Because these three verses are found in other places independent of each other (Matthew 5:15; 10:26; 25:29; Luke 11:33; 12:2; 19:26) they are called "floating sayings." They are strung together here because all three sayings apply to parables and the hearing of parables. Verse 16 can mean that even though parables may take some thinking about, their purpose is to illumine, not to obscure. Verse 17 assures the reader that all will become known in time. Verse 18 is a warning to listen, to dig, to question as the disciples did. Those who are aware of their ignorance will gain great insights, while those who already think they know everything and, therefore, do not bother to listen, will end up knowing nothing.

## FOR FURTHER STUDY AND REFLECTION

### Memory Bank

1. Any or all of the sayings of Jesus are worth committing to memory. Begin with the "Blessings and Woes," Luke 6:20-26, or the sayings in 6:37, 38.

### Research

1. Read more about the form and interpretation of parables in a Bible dictionary article on "Parables."

### Reflection

1. Reread the parables discussed in this session. What does each parable say to you? What is it saying for your life? Be careful not to trivialize the message by making it "helpful hints for better living."

## SUMMARY

As Jesus' long journey to Jerusalem begins, he sends out ahead of him seventy missionaries who are instructed to heal the sick and proclaim the kingdom of God. They return successful, and Jesus rejoices.

Among the teachings of Jesus in this session are lessons about discipleship, the Lord's Prayer, plus the parables of the Good Samaritan and the Friend at Midnight.

Jesus also meets with his friends Mary and Martha as well as critics, including people in the crowd, Pharisees, and scribes.

## BASIC BIBLE REFERENCES

Luke 9:51-62
     10:1-42
     11:1-36
1 Kings 19:19-21
2 Kings 1:9-12
Matthew 6:9-15

## WORD LIST

Samaritan
Pentateuch
hallowed
doxology

*7*

# *The Journey to Jerusalem Begins*

## The Journey Begins

In this narrative Luke has linked a number of sayings and incidents, tying them together as a single journey. The topographical inconsistencies in the story are clues that this is the case. Jesus and the Twelve set out from Galilee and take the short route by going through Samaria. But they arrive in Jerusalem by the long route, through Jericho. In between, Jesus visits the home of Mary and Martha, which (according to John) is in Bethany, only a few miles from Jerusalem. Later Jesus and his disciples are back on the border between Samaria and Galilee.

In addition, this journey does not fit with Mark's general outline, which Luke has followed to this point. Luke departs from Mark at 9:51 and does not return to it until 18:15. A great deal of the material in this large section is unique to Luke. Other parts are common to Matthew, but many of them are in an order different from Matthew's. It would seem that Luke has placed this material in the context of a journey in order to remind the reader again and again that in everything Jesus says and does he is conscious of constantly moving toward the final conflict with sin and death.

Jesus traveled about a great deal during his ministry, and much of what we have here probably happened on the road. There was a real journey to Jerusalem (in John's Gospel there are several), but the order of events on that final trip is most likely not that of Luke's Gospel. Luke is arranging the historical material at his disposal to show the deeper implications of what is happening. Every word and each deed of Jesus is indeed moving him closer and closer to that final confrontation with evil, a confrontation that surely happened in Jerusalem.

## *Rejection and Acceptance*

Luke is fond of arranging the incidents he recounts in complementary or contrasting pairs of stories. The journey narrative opens with contrasting stories about those who do not want Jesus around and those who want to go with Jesus. Read **9:51-56**. There is no doubt that Jerusalem is to be the place where everything will come to a climax. In 13:33 Jesus speaks, perhaps sarcastically, of the necessity of a prophet's dying in Jerusalem. In 18:31 he reminds the disciples that they are on the way to the holy city in order that the Scriptures about him may be fulfilled. In 19:11 the people suppose that *the kingdom of God was to appear immediately* because Jesus was nearing Jerusalem.

The journey begins with a story about Jesus' rejection by a Samaritan village. Judean Jews viewed the Samaritans as descendants of colonists of mixed race who came into Samaria after the fall of the Northern Kingdom in 722 B.C. The Samaritans claimed to follow the Jewish religion, but the Judean Jews believed this was only a superficial cover for heretical religion. The Samaritans built a temple on Mt. Gerizim, believing that to be the proper place for worship. They also had a slightly different version of the Pentateuch (the first five books of the Old Testament, the Law). The Samaritans claimed to be descendants of native Israelites. They insisted that the temple in Jerusalem was not the real temple. Much vilification of each group by the other had gone on over the centuries. By the first century A.D. politics and racism had driven a huge wedge between Samaritans and Jews, making them sworn enemies. The Samaritans certainly had no love for Jewish pilgrims headed for Jerusalem. But according to Luke, it was the fact that Jesus' *face was set toward Jerusalem,* not his race, that made them reject this particular Jew within their territory.

It is interesting that Jesus was planning to enter Samaritan territory and lodge with the people there. This was not at all typical among Jews. Jewish travelers commonly walked all the way around the perimeter of Samaritan territory to avoid contact. Luke does not say that all Samaritans rejected Jesus, only one town. Jesus and his disciples went on to *another village* which might also have been in Samaria. Luke tells us on a number of occasions that Samaritans often received Jesus and his disciples.

The reaction of James and John to the villagers' rejection of Jesus is reminiscent of an Elijah story. Read **2 Kings 1:9-12**. Elijah is alluded to a number of times in Luke. Some people thought that Jesus was Elijah returned. Since the prophet was commonly considered to be the forerunner of the Messiah, his appearance would signal the time of the Messiah's coming. In this situation, Jesus makes it clear to his disciples that there is a new way to deal with enemies. Jesus supersedes the old ways, even those of Elijah. Luke uses the language of exorcism as Jesus upbraids James and John for their desire for revenge. The spirit they display is not from God.

## *Would-Be Disciples*

Luke follows this rejection story with an incident concerning a man who wants to follow Jesus. See **9:57-62**. Jesus answers him with a warning to be clear about the hardships that following him entails. Luke does not tell us whether or not the man was put off by such a warning. A second man is called by Jesus, but this would-be disciple asks leave to bury his father. The third wants to say farewell to his family.

Compare these stories with **1 Kings 19:19-21**. Here Elijah allows Elisha to say good-bye to his parents before becoming Elijah's disciple. Not so with Jesus. Answering the call to discipleship from Jesus must take precedence above all other loyalties. It is only when the summons to follow is answered first that all other loyalties find their true place. When loyalty to any good thing, even family, is valued above God, an idol is created and the right relationship with God and with others is destroyed. Temptation is not just deciding between good and bad but especially between what is good and what is best.

## *The Mission of the Seventy*

Read **10:1-12**. Jesus sends out advance men *to every town and place where he himself intended to go.* The number seventy may be significant because Moses had seventy elders to help him (see Numbers 11:16-25) or because of the seventy nations of the world mentioned in Genesis 10. Jesus does not act impulsively. He plans ahead and sends his emissaries to make preparations (see also 19:29-31 and 22:7-9). The mission of the seventy is twofold: 1) heal any who are ill; 2) proclaim that the *kingdom of God has come near to you.*

## *Woes to the Unrepentant Cities*

In **10:13-16** Jesus declares disaster for three Israelite cities: Chorazin, Bethsaida, and Capernaum. There is no record that he ever visited Chorazin, a town north of Capernaum. Since the Gospels frequently do not mention the site of Jesus' deeds and teachings, this should not be surprising. The assumption quite clearly is that Jesus did great things in each town, and that in each town there was a general failure to repent. These towns were given a wonderful opportunity, but each failed to respond. Note that Jesus pronounces the woes against the towns, not against a few sinful individuals. For the Jews, and for Scripture in general, it is the whole community of faith that is central, not the actions or rights of individuals.

## *The Return of the Seventy*

Continue with **10:17-24**. Even though the exorcism of demons was not part of their instructions, exorcisms are all that the disciples report. Jesus responds that he has witnessed the powers of evil falling. In all the healings and the mercy to sinners Jesus sees the reign of God beginning on earth. The total defeat of Satan (evil) is completely assured.

The disciples are almost drunk with their new-found power and success. Jesus warns them not to take pride in what has happened. Any sense of self-congratulation is inappropriate for disciples. Their joy should be in the fact that God has accepted them. It would become sin if, when the disciples declare, *Lord, in your name even the demons submit to us!* the emphasis were on the "us."

Jesus *rejoiced in the Holy Spirit* and gave thanks to God for reversing human categories; for it is the intellectual infants, not those who think they are wise in theology, who have seen the power of God. The recognition of Jesus as Son of God comes not through knowledge but through God's grace.

## *Doing and Listening*

Luke's next two incidents illustrate the necessity of action as well as knowledge, and of knowledge as well as action. The first account is the occasion of the telling of the parable of the Good Samaritan. Its purpose is to show the nature of the citizens of God's kingdom.

Read the parable in **10:25-37**. Jesus is approached by a lawyer of the Torah. He, presumably, is an expert on the Law of God. He asks Jesus the way to eternal life, not because he seeks to know, but because he already "knows" and wants to see how Jesus will answer. Luke tells us that this is a "test" or trap. Jesus takes the question and throws it back at the lawyer, who then must recite like a child at school. Jesus agrees with the answer and says *do this and you will live.* The doing brings life.

The lawyer's question *And who is my neighbor?* is an inappropriate question for those in the kingdom. The question implies a desire to select some to be neighbors and to reject others. Jesus does not answer this question. Instead the parable of the Good Samaritan answers the question which the lawyer should have asked: "What must I do to be acting like a neighbor?"

In storytelling the "rule of three" is common. The first two characters to come on stage give the expected response. The third character provides a new response. Since the first two in this parable are a priest and a Levite who both fail to help, the audience will expect the third character to be a good Jewish layman who does help, thus making it a parable against religious professionals. Instead, Jesus makes the hero a ceremonially unclean social outcast and religious heretic; a despised Samaritan. The one who represents the way of God's kingdom is not the one who knows the right answers, but the one who does the right actions–the actions of love and mercy. When the lawyer is forced to admit that it is the Samaritan who acts as neighbor, he cannot bring himself to say the word "Samaritan." He says instead, *The one who showed him mercy.* Jesus' closing instruction to the lawyer is *go and do.*

## Mary and Martha

In contrast, Luke next lays before us a story about Mary and Martha, two friends of Jesus, who are found also in John's Gospel. Read Luke **10:38-42**. Martha is a doer and Mary is a thinker. But here Jesus does not commend Martha. Nor does he chastise Mary by telling her to get up and help her sister. Martha's doing is not kingdom action. She may originally have intended the preparation of the meal as an act of love, but she has become *distracted by her many tasks* and is now irritated. Her actions no longer mirror life under the reign of God. What she does, she does because it is a burdensome duty. This is made visible by her anger at her sister and even, perhaps, her irritation at Jesus for allowing Mary to sit while she works.

At some point Mary, along with everyone else, will have to get up and do. But she now is doing the right thing by listening first to Jesus. That is the "one thing needful." Whereas the lawyer was all learning and no action, Martha is all action and no learning. There must be a balance.

There is an additional important feature to this story of Mary and Martha. Martha is the homeowner. No brother Lazarus is mentioned. Jesus is received into a woman's home and teaches a woman. The rabbis did not allow women to be disciples, to "sit at their feet." Jesus not only allows it, but encourages it and commends Mary for her discipleship. Time and again Jesus breaks with social conventions that place people into a hierarchy of importance. In 8:1-3 Luke has told us that Jesus had women disciples who sometimes traveled with him and the other disciples.

## The Lord's Prayer

The Lord's Prayer is found in two places in the New Testament; read **Luke 11:1-4** and **Matthew 6:9-15**. It is also recorded in the *Didache,*[1] a first-century handbook for the Christian Church. Matthew's longer version is more familiar than Luke's simpler text. Luke's version consists of a one-word address followed by five petitions, with no ending doxology.

Below is a literal translation of Luke 11:2-4:

> When you pray, say:
> Father, may your name be hallowed;
> May your reign come;
> Our bread for tomorrow give us day by day;
> And forgive us our sins,
>   for we ourselves also forgive everyone
>   who is indebted to us;
> And do not bring us into testing.

In the Old Testament God is occasionally addressed as "father" (see Deuteronomy 32:6, Isaiah 63:16, Malachi 2:10), but in prayer God is more often referred to as "king." "Father" refers to the creative power of God but also to God as protector of those who are loved. Since humans are made in God's image (Genesis 1:26), "father" also shows an intimate relationship between people and God. Jesus' constant use of the word "father" for God put unusual emphasis on these attributes of God. (God's maternal attributes appear in other contexts.)

The first petition is "Father, may your name be hallowed." Hallowed means holy, sacred, to be treated with ultimate respect.[2] This petition is in the passive voice, a reverent way of praying when God is the subject, the one doing the actions. God will make the holy name respected and sacred by what God does. It is also a prayer that God be worshipped as sovereign–the one who is ultimately respected. Perhaps this hallowing of God's name will come at the eschaton, when God is revealed to the world as sovereign. There is an eschatological sense throughout the Lord's Prayer. And yet, God's name is hallowed when God's love is revealed through the actions of God's faithful people. Jesus' life hallows God's name.

---

1 Pronounced "did-ah-kay," a Greek word for "teaching."

2 On this and all the petitions, see the Kerygma publication *Lord, Teach Us To Pray.*

The second petition is much the same: "May your reign come." The coming of God's rule ("the kingdom"), the eschaton in its fullness, is the ultimate hallowing of God's name, when God rules in every heart and God's will is done completely. It is important to note that the reign will be brought in by God, not by us. There can be, then, no doubt that it will come. Matthew's addition may *your will be done on earth, as it is in heaven* is another way of saying the same thing. "Your reign come" means that God will rule on this earth as completely as God rules heaven. To pray *your will be done on earth* is the ultimate hallowing of God's name.

In the petitions *give us, forgive us, bring us,* in verses 3-4, the recipient of the action is the petitioner. The third petition is the most difficult to translate. Much of the problem stems from the word traditionally translated "daily." The word does not exist for sure in any other place in ancient Greek writings. Various translations have been used: "lasting," "for our needs," "necessary for existence." "Bread" may stand for all the things we need in order to do God's will. They are given to us new a day at a time.

The fourth petition is the only one with a condition. Making God's forgiveness conditional on our forgiving has no real parallel in Jewish prayers. The Lord's Prayer in Matthew is followed by a warning to take this petition seriously (6:14-15. See also 18:23-35). The yoking of God's action to our action has occurred previously in Luke 6:37-38a. The words "sins," "debts," and "trespasses" (the last picked up from Matthew 6:14) are interchangeable here. The petition asks God to forgive us, most likely on the final Judgment Day, for we continually forgive others in our daily lives. Aside from conditioned forgiveness, this is a very Jewish prayer.

The final petition seems strange to many people, for it seems to assume that God desires to lead us into temptation! The word translated "temptation" usually means "testing." The temptation, for most people, is to quit when the going gets tough. Jesus in Gethsemane tells the disciples to pray that they *may not come into the time of trial* (Luke 22:40, 46). It does not have the meaning of enticing us to commit sin, but rather of keeping us from being tested to the point where we would renounce our Lord. The flavor of it may be found in the words of the hymn *O Sacred Head, Now Wounded:* "O make me thine forever; and should I fainting be, Lord, let me never, never outlive my love to thee."

The doxology, "For thine is the kingdom and the power and the glory forever," was added to Matthew's text at an early date. It also appears in a somewhat different form in the *Didache.* It is a fitting ending to the prayer and completely in line with Jewish and Christian thought concerning the power and the glory of God. [3]

---

3  These words do not appear in many Bibles because they are not included in the best manuscripts of Matthew.

## *Words of Assurance*

Luke concludes this section on prayer with the parable of the Friend at Midnight and sayings concerning God's faithfulness. Read **11:5-13**. The parable presupposes a knowledge of Palestinian village life. A village family would all sleep in one room on mats on the floor. A bar would be put across the door. Thus getting up to help a friend would mean the inconveniencing of the entire family. Three loaves of bread were considered a meal for one person. Loaning the loaves would not be a hardship, for fresh loaves were baked each morning. It was unthinkable for a person to refuse hospitality to visitors. The friend who is banging on the door is in desperate circumstances. He must have food for his guest. It would, therefore, be unacceptable for the homeowner to refuse to help his friend even if it means inconvenience. The construction of verse 7 implies that no decent person would give such an answer. Jesus' hearers would find that behavior outrageous. The "I can't" means "I won't." And even, for the sake of argument, if someone would say such a thing, he would still eventually get up and help because of the other's persistence.

Jesus is not saying that God is like a bad neighbor who must be badgered into helping. Rather he is arguing from the lesser to the greater. If any right-thinking person would act thus, how much more will God do what is right. There is absolutely no doubt that the disciples' prayers will be answered. We can be persistent in prayer because we know without doubt that God will hear. The true focus of this parable is the sureness of the answer. It gives the great assurance of the goodness of God.

Luke follows the Friend at Midnight with sayings of Jesus which make the same point. Any question that begins "Which of you" will receive either the answer "everyone" or "no one." In this case the answer Jesus expects is clearly "no one." No father present would give his child a poisonous snake or a scorpion when the child asks for food. If sinful humans would not do such a thing, why do the hearers have so much trouble trusting God who is good?

Whereas Matthew reads *good things* (7:11) Luke has *the Holy Spirit* (verse 13). The object of prayer is not things, but God's presence with us. For Luke, the Holy Spirit is the prime necessity. It is the power of Jesus Christ and the creator of the Church. The Gospel of Luke ends with Jesus instructing the disciples to wait for the *power from on high* (24:49). Luke's book of Acts begins with the Holy Spirit creating the Church.

## Controversy

Read **11:14-23**. Beelzebul means "lord of the house." He was the god of the Philistine city of Ekron (2 Kings 1:2). The name can be corrupted to "Beelzebub" which means "lord of the flies." In Aramaic Beelzebul can also be interpreted "lord of dung." Neither of these names is a name for Satan. Here, however, Beelzebul is identified as *the ruler of the demons.*

Jesus counters the charge that his power is demonic: 1) The charge is not logical. Why would demons expel demons? 2) The exorcists of (presumably) the Pharisees know that only God can destroy evil, so their own experts would condemn them for blasphemy; 3) Jesus' works show that the kingdom of God is invading the kingdom of evil and destroying it. How can Jesus' enemies deny it?

The *strong man* in verse 21 is Satan, the power of evil. The "lord of the house" is being attacked by *one stronger,* Jesus, the power of God. All Beelzebul's weapons are being destroyed. What the people are witnessing in Jesus' healings is the invasion of evil's domain by the power of God. There is no question as to the outcome. God is the *one stronger.* Nowhere in the Scriptures is there ever the slightest indication that the powers of evil are even remotely equal to the power of God. The outcome of this confrontation is never in doubt.

## A Demon and Its Friends

Now read **11:24-28**. A disembodied demon was thought to inhabit desert areas, *waterless regions.* This demon has been exorcised from a person, leaving that person "clean and all fixed up" (TEV). But if that person does not replace the exorcised evil with the positive power of God's love, that one remains empty. A life full of "thou shalt nots" and concerned only with avoiding evil is an empty life. It leaves plenty of room for the demon not only to return, but to bring seven other spirits to join it. In Judaism, seven was a number that signified completeness. The possessed man's situation is now impossible. He is completely possessed. Had his life been filled with God's love and the deeds of love, there would have been no abiding place for evil. Exorcism is not enough.

Jesus' response to the woman in verses 27-28 reinforces this understanding. Blessedness is found in hearing and doing God's word. The positive ethical dimension, which is a major theme in Luke, is sounded again and again.

## *Demand for a Miracle*

Continue on to **11:29-32**. Miracles do not produce faith. Miracles are signs of the presence of the kingdom of God, but they are only seen as such by those who already have faith. Others, such as the Pharisees and lawyers, can see miracle after miracle and still fail to believe. Miracles can be explained away. The demand for such signs only shows, says Jesus, that the people asking for them are evil. They do not trust the word of God but demand that God jump through their hoops to prove that God is God.

The sign of Jonah is Jonah's preaching of repentance. The people of Nineveh repented at the preaching of Jonah. But when Jesus himself preaches repentance, the crowd, instead of repenting, demands signs. The queen of Sheba (2 Chronicles 9:1-12) went to great lengths to hear Solomon and was impressed. These people hear Jesus and demand proof.

## *Light*

Finally, read **11:33-36**. This little section on light is composed of three formerly independent sayings: verses 33, 34-35, and 36. Jesus' message is clear to persons of integrity ("sound eye"). But those who refuse to see are not going to see. No amount of miracles will give them light.

### FOR FURTHER STUDY AND REFLECTION

#### Memory Bank

1. Memorize Luke's version of the Lord's Prayer. Use it from time to time in your private devotions.

#### Research

1. Use a Bible dictionary, an encyclopedia, or other reference book to learn more about the district of Samaria and/or the people of Samaria. Also include the Samaritan temple and the Samaritan faith.

2. Locate Samaria, Galilee, Nazareth, Judea, and Jerusalem on a map of Palestine in New Testament times. Trace locations on Jesus' journey as outlined by Luke.

**Reflection**

1. In your own life how balanced are listening and doing? Are you more like the lawyer looking for a loophole to escape the demands of the gospel, or like Martha constantly doing but feeling used and unappreciated? Do you need to restore a balance? If so, how?

## SUMMARY

Jesus' journey to Jerusalem continues. An attack on the hypocrisy of the Pharisees and lawyers, who pretend to be religious, leads to warnings to the disciples not to deny their faith during times of persecution.

The subject of all of chapter 12 and part of 13 is the crises that Jesus' presence is bringing. There are warnings about possessions, the temptations to abuse authority, watchfulness, and bearing fruit. Jesus speaks of his own crisis hour and the crisis hour for Israel.

## BASIC BIBLE REFERENCES

Luke 11:37-53
12:1-59
13:1-9

## WORD LIST

parousia
Gehenna
Ecclesiasticus

*8*

# Warnings on
# the Journey

## *Jesus' Accusations*

Begin your study with **11:37-53**. Luke reminds us that Jesus and the Pharisees were not always enemies. Jesus accepts dinner invitations to the homes of Pharisees. Jesus' failure to wash his hands had nothing to do with cleanliness or good hygiene–the first century knew nothing of germs. Hand washing was a ritual observed rather elaborately by the Pharisees, although it was nowhere prescribed by the Law. The scribes had made it an important practice (see Mark 7:1-4). The host's amazement at Jesus' omission of this ritual may indicate that Jesus was known to usually observe Jewish ritual. Jesus is not an outsider in his debates with the Pharisees and scribes but rather one who loves his religion and would defend it against those who twist it.

Jesus utters two woes against the Pharisees. First, he accuses them of concentrating on ritual purity–characterized by such things as the ceremonial washing of vessels–while neglecting the cleansing of their hearts. They are scrupulous in their observance of the Law to the point of tithing the herbs in their kitchen gardens, but *neglect justice and the love of God.* They have convinced themselves that because they are so observant of ritual they are thereby very religious. But they have missed the heart of their religion entirely. Note that Jesus is not condemning religious ritual. He is warning against letting ritual observances become a substitute for serving God with one's whole heart and soul.

Secondly, Jesus denounces the Pharisees for using their religion as a means of elevating themselves in the eyes of others. They covet respect and places of honor in God's house because of their pious ways. They love the appearance of holiness, but their hearts are not holy. The comment in 11:44 about *unmarked graves* is a reference to the thought that contact with dead bodies or graves made one ritually unclean. In sum, the only acceptable reason for being religious is to honor God, and to draw attention to God, never to self.

The scribes (lawyers) take offense at Jesus' attack. Jesus then levies three woes against the scribes. First, they turn the Law into a severe code of "do's" and "don'ts." God gave the Law to be a joy for the people, to light the path of God's people so they would not stumble. (Psalm 119, the longest psalm, is a song of praise to God for the gift of the Law). The scribes, having turned God's word of life into a burden, have no interest in helping the common people to carry this burden. They are content to condemn them as unclean.

Second, the scribes are hypocrites. They praise the prophets of old, but they participate in the same acts of disobedience that destroyed the prophets. The "Wisdom of God" may be a reference to a now lost apocryphal book. Abel is the first murder victim mentioned in the Torah (Genesis 4:8). Zechariah is the last mentioned in the Writings, the end of the Jewish canon (2 Chronicles 24:20-22).

The third woe is the most serious. The scribes, as custodians of God's word, had the key to the knowledge of God. But they have substituted ritual and appearance for the love of God. They have not used the key themselves, and they have made such a travesty of the Law in their interpretations, that they have prevented the people from knowing God as well. That is a great condemnation.

The response of the scribes and Pharisees is not unexpected. They follow Jesus into the street still arguing. They have not taken to heart anything that he has said. They are only interested in discrediting him by trapping him in his own words.

## *Two Kinds of Hypocrisy*

The Pharisees and lawyers who oppose Jesus are hypocrites because they make a show of being religious when in truth they are very far from God. But there is a form of hypocrisy that is every bit as dangerous. Jesus warns his disciples about the hypocrisy of being his followers but pretending not to be.

Now read **12:1-12**. The kingdom will unveil all truth. Those who have denied Jesus in order to save their skins will not be able to hide their hypocrisy. (These verses spoke very strongly to the church of Luke's day, which was beginning to experience persecution.) Jesus speaks of *those who kill the body* and of being *brought before the synagogues, the rulers, and the authorities.* These things did not happen to the disciples until after the resurrection.

The word in verse 5 translated "hell" is "Gehenna" in the Greek text. Gehenna or the "Valley of Hinnom" is a ravine south of Jerusalem. In ancient times children had been sacrificed there to the god Molech (Jeremiah 7:31; 2 Chronicles 28:3). During Jesus' time Gehenna was a dump where garbage was burned. For a hundred years before Jesus the name had been used metaphorically to denote the place of punishment of the wicked.

No punishment inflicted by humans can compare with being cast away from God. Death is preferable to separation from God. This warning is contrasted with the words *do not be afraid.* Those who put their trust in God's love need not be afraid of the awesome power of God.

The Holy Spirit will be the defender and teacher of the disciples to enable them to speak the truth and not falter. Luke's book of Acts contains several accounts of the Holy Spirit's presence during the church's persecutions (for example Acts 7:55-56). What does Jesus mean by blaspheming *against the Holy Spirit?* In its context here it may mean to deny the presence of the Holy Spirit in one's life by denying one's discipleship. To cut oneself off from the Holy Spirit is to choose death. The disciples of Jesus must never deny the Holy Spirit by renouncing their faith in the face of persecutions.

## *Warnings About Greed*

The warnings against hypocrisy are followed by warnings against greed and against putting faith in that which cannot save. Read **12:13-21**. The parable of the Rich Fool is unique to Luke. It is one of several parables in Luke where the rich or powerful are condemned for their selfish actions (see also 7:41-42: 16:19-31).

The occasion for the parable is important. A man in the crowd cries out to Jesus to act as a mediator or judge in a financial situation. His cry would be regarded by those around him as a cry for justice. Jesus answers with words reminiscent of Exodus 2:14, where Moses is accused of acting as a judge unbidden. [Moses later became the judge and divider over Israel (Exodus 18:13)]. Jesus here rejects the role of judge and divider.

Jesus' response to the man is a warning to be on guard against greed. The words alert the hearers that a real danger is lurking in greed. The word used in verse 15 for greed means "insatiability"; whatever one has is never quite enough. The warning is to avoid falling into the trap of thinking, "If I just had …, I would be happy." Life is not found in piling up things.

The parable of the Rich Fool is found in outline form in chapter 11 of the apocryphal book *Ecclesiasticus*, sometimes called *Ben Sirach*. Jesus develops a more complete story in his parable. There is no indication that the rich man is a thief or unscrupulous; Jesus simply says that his land *produced abundantly*. It is not how he came to be rich that gives him trouble. It is the way he uses what he has. His conversation with himself is revealing. There is no question at any point of using even a portion of his goods on behalf of anyone but himself. He speaks of *my crops, my barns, my goods, my soul*. It is about to become painfully clear to him that, in reality, he does not "own" crops, barns, goods, or his own soul. The fool's recommendation to himself in verse 19 is an ascending list: *Relax, eat, drink, be merry.* Jesus is warning not only the man who originally cried for justice, but all those who worry about money and possessions that they are most certainly not on the path to life.

Throughout this story there is a play on words going on in the Greek. Since Jesus told the story in Aramaic, the play on words may be Luke's, but it is instructive nonetheless. The word *abundantly* is *euphoresen*. The word *merry* is *euphron*, which means to expand the diaphragm (the *phron*) as in a sigh of contentment. The rich man believes that his *euphoresen* (abundant yield) brings *euphron* (contentment). The next word is God's: *Fool*, which here is the rare Greek word *aphron,* which literally means "without a diaphragm." He has nothing.[1]

None of the things the rich man has been so concerned with were his. The sense of verse 20 is that the fool's soul is only on loan from God and God is calling in the debt. Without his self, his goods mean nothing (see 9:25). Jesus concludes by reminding the listeners that those who live by the world's standards instead of God's standards are the same kind of

---

1 Background material for this discussion of the parable of the Rich Fool is taken from the audiotape "New Perspectives on the Parables, Volume 1," by Kenneth Bailey, Thesis Tapes, Pittsburgh, Pennsylvania, 1972, side 2.

fools. The only way to be rich in God's sight is to be rich in God's love and compassion, which always shows itself in how we respond to others.

## What, Me Worry?

Continue your study by reading **12:22-34**. (In Matthew this is part of the Sermon on the Mount). As in other "sermons" in Luke, the teaching here is not directed to the crowds but to the disciples. The crowds, however, overhear Jesus' instructions to his followers and thus learn what discipleship would mean for themselves. The first warning (above) had been against covetousness. This warning is against anxiety over money and goods. Jesus here instructs the disciples not to be preoccupied with material things, even necessities such as food and drink. It is not only the dramatic events of life, such as persecution, that tempt disciples, but more subtly, it is the everyday worries and concerns that lead people away from God, that slowly erode faith. Jesus is not saying that we have no need of food, clothes, and the other necessities of life. *Your Father knows that you need them.* The problem is in putting our concern for things ahead of what God wants us to be concerned about. The cure for anxiety and preoccupation with things is to get life into perspective. Our first concern as disciples is to care about doing God's will. Our first priority is God and what God wants us to be concerned with.

Fear and anxiety are the opposites of trust in God. Once again, disciples hear the words, *Do not be afraid.* Jesus calls those who trust him *little flock.* There is a tenderness and a gentleness for those who follow him. There is no need to wring our hands over our lives, *for it is your Father's good pleasure to give you the kingdom.* The doors of the kingdom of God stand wide open to those who put their trust in God, not in the false security of a warehouse of stockpiled goodies. Take note of 12:34. It does not read, "Where your heart is, there will your treasure be also." The warning is to be careful about what you treasure, for your heart, your devotion, your concern, will automatically be there as well.

## The Waiting Servants

In its present form the story in **12:35-40** is a parable about discipleship. The servants are disciples of Jesus who are waiting for the "parousia," the Lord's return. The message is to be ready, no matter how much the return may be delayed. Those who keep uppermost in their minds the fact that the Lord is coming will be the ones who remember that they are servants. Their actions will, therefore, constitute their preparation for the Lord's return.

They will be *dressed for action.* They will not be mentally and spiritually asleep, but will have *their lamps lit.*

This is a positive parable, for it speaks of ready servants who will be blessed. They will also receive an amazing gift: the Master will serve them at table! No master ever so honored his servants. But Jesus will do precisely that (see 22:27, also John 13:1-11).

Since there are no quotation marks in the Greek manuscripts, some people have suggested that verses 39-40 could be Luke's own reminder to the church of his day. The phrase *Son of Man,* however, is almost always used by Jesus himself. In any case, the words carry the same message to Jesus' disciples in all circumstances: we do not know when the Master will return, so we must live in readiness at all times.

## Faithful and Unfaithful Servants

Next read **12:41-48**. This parable deals with servants who have been entrusted with authority. The words could apply to the scribes. "The scribes and the Pharisees are the authorized interpreters of Moses' Law" (Matthew 23:2 TEV). In that case, Jesus sees them as those who betrayed their sacred trust from God. Instead of helping God's children with God's gift of the Law, the leaders have imposed the Law as a burden and used it to condemn as worthless those outside their circle. All this they have done while acting as their Master's servants.

The early church would take this warning to heart. Church leaders have been entrusted with the gospel message of God. If they, like the scribes and Pharisees before them, misuse their authority and power, they can expect no lighter punishment. Power and authority provide their own temptations. Those with power to act and authority to speak will have to show great strength and obedience to avoid failing. Jesus ends this section with a proverb.

## The Time is Coming

Read **12:49-53**. *I came to bring fire to the earth, and how I wish it were already kindled!* The words show the deep feelings Jesus has as he realizes that the critical moment is almost upon him, upon Israel, and ultimately upon the world. The fire that Jesus will set is the fire of judgment and of purification (Malachi 3:2-3). That fire will be set by the death of Jesus, which is symbolized in the *baptism* Jesus awaits. When that time comes, *the inner thoughts* *of many* (Luke 2:35) will be revealed. Each one must then declare his or her loyalty, bringing divisions even among family members. But discipleship, loyalty to Jesus, goes beyond family loyalties. Jesus has come not to bring a peace that is only the containment of hostilities. Jesus' peace is positive goodwill. It is for those who follow him. There is no peace for those whose hearts and minds are at war with God.

## *Understanding the Time*

Now read **12:54-56**. As in previous passages, the vague introduction that Luke gives to this section tells us that it is not necessarily connected to the others. These verses are directed to the crowd. We can almost hear the anger and frustration in Jesus' voice. Everyone can read the signs of changing weather, but no one seems to be able to see the sign of God–the ministry of Jesus in their midst. *The present time* is a wake-up call to put one's relationship right with God, and fast! That relationship is lived out in signs of love and hope given to neighbors.

In **12:57-59**, Jesus warns his hearers that since God is in the right, we would be fools to try to press our case in God's court (the eschaton). Better to repent now (settle out of court) than to await the time when all that will be left is the sentencing. The time to seek God's mercy is now. To wait means that we will have our entire debt to God to pay.

## *Repent or Perish*

The final section for this chapter is **13:1-9**. This passage is unique to Luke. It deals with one of Luke's primary themes, repentance. Again, Luke sets his material in contrasting patterns. The image of judgment, which has just been discussed, is followed by a call to repent or perish. This call will be followed by a short parable on God's patience (verses 6-9). Luke intends to hold in tension God's mercy and God's judgment, God's grace and the need for us to repent now. These things do not cancel each other out; they are paradoxes that must all be dealt with.

Two events form the basis of the discussion. The first is brought up by some people who want to know why the innocent suffer. They relate the story of those killed in the very act of prayer. Although the people do not put the question to Jesus, he knows why they are concerned. *Do you think that because these Galileans suffered in this way they were worse sinners than all other Galileans?* The idea had been prevalent in Israel for centuries that in this life sinners are punished and the good prosper. Certainly it was obvious that many times people's sins brought down evil upon their own heads. It was also obvious that many times people who did right seemed to be rewarded.

From there it was a small jump in thought to assume that all the evils that befell a person were punishment for some sin–"What did I do to deserve this?"–all good fortune a reward. The crowds in John's Gospel ask Jesus, *Who sinned, this man or his parents, that he was born blind?* (9:2). Even a newborn must have been a sinner, since he was born blind! Several texts in the Old Testament, such as Psalm 1, tend to support this view. The book of Job and other Old Testament writings, such as Psalm 73, however, refuse to accept this kind of thinking. The common people of Jesus' day, as well as the Pharisees, believed that the poor, the ill, those who suffered tragedies, and the handicapped were being punished by God for some sin. One of the Pharisees' "proofs" of their righteousness was the fact that no one who was physically imperfect was allowed into their group.

Jesus countered this way of thinking from the very first. He announced that it was to proclaim God's good news to the poor, the blind, and the oppressed that he had come (Luke 4:18-19). He went out to those who were "accursed" according to the Pharisees and brought them into the kingdom. Finally, as the ultimate innocent, Jesus himself suffered death by state execution. In no way can followers of Jesus feel justified in believing that tragedy or poverty is a punishment for sin–or that good luck and wealth are a reward from God.

Jesus answers the unspoken question of the people concerning the death of the Galileans: *No.* He then turns the discussion into a warning about the sureness of the destruction of anyone who will not repent. Jesus himself brings up another example, one which we might call a natural disaster. Again his answer is *No,* they were no worse people than anyone else. And again Jesus uses the opportunity to warn all his listeners to think about what will happen to each of them if they remain stubbornly opposed to repenting.

## *The Barren Fig Tree*

Luke concludes this section with Jesus' parable of the Barren Fig Tree. Read **13:6-9** again. A fig tree takes three years to reach maturity. Presumably the owner has been patient an additional three years, waiting for this mature tree to produce. Good soil is at a premium in Israel. No one can afford to waste it with unfruitful trees. The gardener buys time for the tree with a promise to mulch around it. He will also put on manure, a most unusual step to take. There is mercy in God's justice. But God's desire for goodness cannot forever be thwarted by those who refuse to repent and produce good fruits. The parable is open-ended. It is the hearers themselves who must write the ending, for it is the hearers themselves who must bear fruit or else be uprooted.

## FOR FURTHER STUDY AND DISCUSSION

### Memory Bank

1. Luke 12:4-7. These verses contain both a warning and words of comfort.

2. 12:34. This verse serves as a reminder to be careful about what we treasure, lest we be tempted away from the true riches.

### Research

1. A parallel to the parable of the fig tree in Luke (13:6-9) is found in Matthew 21:18-20 and Mark 11:12-14. Here Jesus curses the fig tree. Review commentaries on this story. What do you understand Jesus to be doing by this action?

2. Look up the word "parousia" in a Bible dictionary. List the different meanings it may have. How is it most often used in Luke?

### Reflection

1. In the commentary on Luke 12:22-34 it was said, "It is not only the dramatic events of life, such as persecution, that tempt disciples, but more subtly, it is the everyday worries and concerns that lead people away from God …" What in your own life most often tempts you? What rules your life–at least from time to time?

## SUMMARY

As the travel narrative continues, Jesus teaches about life in the kingdom of God, how precious it is, and how life is lived there. Jesus also speaks of what it will cost to enter the kingdom. In this section we find some of Jesus' most famous parables including the Mustard Seed, the Great Dinner, the Lost Sheep, and the Lost Sons.

## BASIC BIBLE REFERENCES

Luke 13:18-35
     14:1-35
     15:1-32

## WORD LIST

Kesassa Ceremony

*9*

# *Life in the Kingdom of God*

## The Kingdom Comes

Begin with **13:18-21**. The parables of the Mustard Seed and of the Yeast make the same point. The phrase *It is like* (verses 19 and 21) really means "It is the case with the kingdom as with …" The kingdom is not being compared to the tiny seed or the bit of yeast, but to the great tree and the huge mass of leavened dough that result from them. The image of a great tree with birds making *nests in its branches* is a familiar symbol in the Old Testament (see Ezekiel 17:22-24; 31:6). It represents a great empire that shelters all people. God will produce his great empire, the reign of God, and all peoples will be at home in God's love. The growth of the tree is owed to no human agency. God will produce the growth. The kingdom is guaranteed because God will bring it to fruition.

A woman puts yeast in *three measures of flour,* which is equivalent to just over a bushel. This would make enough bread for one hundred people, far more than the typical three or four loaves a woman usually baked at a time. The idea of the yeast leavening a bushel of dough and the mustard seed becoming a tree bring an eschatological flavor to these parables. We are dealing here with divine realities. Again, the results do not depend on human agency; leavened dough rises inevitably. So it is with God's reign; it will come without our help. God is the agent behind it.

## Doors, Narrow and Closed

Now read **13:22-30**. In this section, Luke has put together several sayings of Jesus to form one unit. Jesus is asked to respond to the question *Lord, will only a few be saved?* which was not an unusual question in Jesus' day. The question of the number to be saved at the Last Day was debated in late Jewish literature. In 2 Esdras 8:1-3 the answer is: "The Most High made this world for the sake of many, but the world to come, for the sake of few …; many have been created, but few will be saved" (Goodspeed translation). Jesus answers only with a warning about the narrow door, which should probably be understood as an encouragement to discipline and a deep desire for God's will.

Then there is the symbol of the closed door marking that time when it will be too late to make a decision to repent and enter the kingdom. The door into the kingdom will be shut. It will not be reopened for those who claim to have an acquaintance with Jesus. In fact, such acquaintance condemns them, for they heard the gospel from him and did not respond. Note that in this parable the Lord of the house is Jesus: *We ate and drank with you, and you taught in our streets.* The warning here is the same as the one in the parable of the Ten Bridesmaids in Matthew 25:1-13. The day is coming when it will be too late to make a decision. The critical time, therefore, is now.

There is a banquet going on in that house with the closed door. In Jesus' parables a meal, party, banquet, or feast always is a reference to the kingdom of God. Table fellowship with God is the greatest party of all, the one thing to aim for, the glorious fulfillment of all creation. But to those who have not repented, who have not responded to the gospel represented in Jesus' ministry, the door to the banquet is shut. And for those in Israel who did not respond, what could be worse than watching not only the great patriarchs of Israel enter the banquet, but Gentiles as well: *Then people will come from east and west, from north and south, and will eat in the kingdom of God.* Verse 30 is a floating saying found in several places in the Gospels. Only Luke uses it to contrast Jews and Gentiles.

## Laments Over Jerusalem

Not all Pharisees were hostile to Jesus. Several invited him to dinner to listen quite honestly to his teaching. In Acts 15:5 Luke reminds us that some Pharisees had become believers. Read **13:31-35**. In this passage, a group of Pharisees comes to warn Jesus about Herod Antipas' death threats against him. Jesus asks them to get a message to Herod for him, a harsh message. In Jewish literature foxes were destructive. In Greek literature they were crafty. Whatever Jesus meant by *fox*, it was clearly not a compliment. Jesus instructs the Pharisees to tell Herod, in essence, that his threats will have no effect at all on his work. The message ends with what might be sarcasm. Jerusalem, the holy city, had long been the place where God's servants had suffered for God's message.

Jerusalem's crisis hour was upon it; the time for decision had come, and Jerusalem went about its business unheeding. Jesus' lament has in it real sadness for a city he loved. The words of verse 35b are almost identical to the words the crowds will use on Palm Sunday.

## More Table Talk

Read **14:1-14**. The healing of the man with dropsy is initiated by Jesus himself. It is an occasion not only for mercy, but for instructing the Pharisees. Here it is Jesus who raises the issue of working on the Sabbath. The scribes and Pharisees do not answer, probably because they know the answer which they cannot refute, but which they do not like. Jesus reminds them of the instruction in the Law that allows work in the case of an emergency. He apparently sees the alleviation of human suffering as an emergency. Love for others in the kingdom of God overrides all objections. The Pharisees do not speak at all in this passage.

People have sometimes dismissed verses 7-14 as nothing more than clever words on table manners. These present sayings have no more to do with good table manners than the Parable of the Sower has to do with agriculture. The saying about choosing places at the table is a parable. The reference to a wedding banquet is a clue that what Jesus is talking about is the kingdom of God. Here, then, is a warning to the proud who think that their good behavior, their keeping of the Law, entitles them to a choice place at the messianic banquet. It is a call to beware of self-righteousness and to cultivate a humble spirit in God's presence. Jesus can see from the guests' behavior at dinner *(When he noticed how the guests chose the places of honor ...)* that they have not even begun to look at themselves as God sees them. They are full of pride and arrogance. It is often in the small actions of everyday life that people divulge their true natures.

Jesus has a warning for the host as well as the guests. It is an injunction to use dinner invitations as a way of recalling God's graciousness to all of us, we who can never repay. The instruction to invite social outcasts to lunch is the complete reverse of what a Pharisee would do. This is a list of precisely those people a Pharisee would never dream of inviting. Just so, the host who is himself invited to God's banquet–the kingdom–is a complete social mismatch who can return only gratitude. Life in the kingdom turns human values upside down.

## *The Parable of the Great Dinner*

The parable in **14:15-24** again illustrates the importance of understanding the social customs of the time in order to be able to get the point of the story.[1] The issuing of invitations in ancient, and in some places modern, Middle Eastern societies is not at all like the issuing of invitations in the West. There an invitation is issued only a day or two in advance. The closer to the event the invitation is accepted, the more the guest is bound by courtesy to attend. The host will slaughter a fairly large animal for a banquet and must be sure of the number who will attend, since there is no way to preserve leftover meat. When the dinner has been prepared, those who accepted the invitation are called to come. The meal is ready, the guests are obligated, the party will now commence.

Now the excuses begin, and one and all they are outrageous and insulting. The first excuse is the purchase of a piece of land. In the first place, no one would enter into such a contract when he had already accepted an invitation to a banquet. But secondly, no one in his right mind bought property sight unseen. The purchase of land was a very carefully thought out venture. The potential purchaser would literally go over every square inch. He would know exactly where the water was; he would find out who had farmed it in the past and what the yields had been. The thought that someone had purchased property and <u>Now</u> had to see what it was like was an obvious lie. Jesus' listeners would have been shocked at the insult to the host.

The excuse in verse 19 is even more insulting. Again, the purchase of something so expensive and so important as a yoke of oxen took all day to accomplish. In many markets a small plot of ground was furnished so that potential buyers could try out a pair of animals. The buyer might try different combinations of oxen to see how they pulled together, to match their strength, to see if they could pull straight. The excuse that a man had bought untested not one yoke of oxen, but ten animals, is akin to our saying: "I've bought half a dozen cars. Now I have to go see what kind they are and whether they are new or used." The lie is so obvious as to be a great insult.

---

1 Background material for the parable of the Great Dinner and the parables in Luke 15 is again from Kenneth Bailey's "New Perspectives on the Parables."

Following the rule of three, Jesus saves the worst insult to the host for last. The guest says, *I have just been married, and therefore I cannot come.* This is not even a polite response. There is no apology. But worse than that, he has mentioned a woman (the verse in Greek reads "married a woman"). Middle Eastern men very often even today will not mention their wives or mothers in conversation with other men, and certainly not ever to a servant. It is not chauvinism so much as respect for the woman's privacy. The marriage, moreover, is certainly a lie, for no village could have both a banquet and a wedding feast at the same time. Each host would want all the leading citizens at his feast. Two feasts at the same time in a village of 150 to 300 people simply did not happen. In addition, he could never have accepted the banquet invitation if he had been about to marry. This is the most flagrant and insulting of all the lies. What the guest really means is, "I've got someone in the back room. Go away." A Palestinian audience would have been thoroughly shocked.

It is no surprise that the host becomes angry. Since every reference to a banquet in Jesus' parables is a symbol for the great party that is life in the kingdom of God, the host here is God. The insulting, would-be guests are the Pharisees and those others who, by their religion, have accepted the invitation to the banquet. Now, however, when called to the great feast of God, their lame, insulting excuses about Sabbath observance and complaints about their dinner companions are as insulting as the excuses of the guests in Jesus' parable.

The order goes out from God to bring *the poor, the crippled, the blind, and the lame* to the party. These are the outcasts of Israel whom Jesus has called. The order is obeyed, but still there is room. The servants are sent *into the roads and lanes,* out beyond Israel to the Gentiles.

A note of explanation is necessary concerning verse 23. It was on this verse that the rationale for the medieval Inquisition was based: *compel people to come in.* In the Middle East of the first century, status was very important. If a person of lower status was invited by his better to a social event, he had to make a great show of his unworthiness saying things such as, "Oh, no, I couldn't. It's so kind of you to offer, but I'd be totally out of my depth. I simply couldn't." The would-be host would have to counter with all kinds of begging and cajoling in order to convince the guest that the host was not merely being polite. A host might all but drag a guest into the house.

As in 13:28-29, those who would have been guests are outside, and the despised are honored guests. Here is another crisis parable as Jesus warns the religious to stop making foolish excuses before it is too late.

## *The Cost of Discipleship*

In contrast to the warning not to be left out of the banquet, the next section contains warnings by Jesus to count the cost of discipleship. What will it cost to become a follower of Jesus? To enter the kingdom of God? The answer is "Precisely everything." Becoming a disciple is not a step to be taken lightly, for it will change every relationship we have. Read **14:25-33**. The most precious relationship most people have is with their families. But even this relationship cannot supersede loyalty and love to God. If it does, it becomes an idol. God is first or not in the picture at all.

The word *hate* in verse 26 has confused many readers. In Matthew the phrase is *loves father or mother more than me* (10:37a). The word "hate" cannot mean here what it does in the sentence "I hate you!" That would contradict the rest of Jesus' teachings about love of neighbor and caring for the members of one's family. We are also called to love our neighbors as we love ourselves. We cannot both hate and love ourselves! It may be that hate is a Semitic expression here meaning to be detached from another, so that when it is necessary to choose, God's kingdom will always come first. At the most, it may be hyperbole for the sake of shocking contrast. Without love for God all other loves, even love of family and self, degenerate into self-centeredness, manipulation, and idolatry.

The twin parables of the Tower Builder and the King Preparing for Battle are both warnings not to embark on the way of discipleship until one understands exactly what it will cost. This is no place for the faint hearted. Those who make the decision give up everything but discover that they have lost nothing.

Read **14:34-35**. The saying about salt may seem out of place. But if disciples are like salt, then a disciple without devotion to Christ is like salt without saltiness; it is nothing.

## *Lost and Found*

The three parables that constitute chapter 15 share a common theme: God's joy over the safe return of God's own lost children. Read **15:1-7**. In Matthew's version of the Lost Sheep

(18:12-14) the parable is addressed to Jesus' disciples. In Luke it is addressed to the Pharisees and the scribes, where it has become a defense of the gospel and Jesus' ministry. The shepherd in Jesus' day might have been part owner of a flock or someone hired by the village to watch their collective flock. The shepherd is responsible for the flock. Jesus here is making a subtle comparison with the Pharisees and scribes, who are responsible for God's flock.

Jesus asks what any reasonable, self-respecting shepherd would do if he were to be so careless as to lose a sheep. He then goes on to give the answer: he will leave the ninety-nine with his assistants and go off into the wilds searching for the sheep until he finds it. And when he does, he is so full of joy that the lost is safely found, that he is willing to walk all the rocky way home with a fifty-pound sheep on his shoulders. The clear implication for the Pharisees and scribes is that they, the shepherds of God's flock, have lost sheep right and left and have not even tried to bring them back. And when Jesus goes out to do their job for them, they do not rejoice, they complain! But God rejoices, and that rejoicing defines life in the kingdom of God. Later rabbis would discuss whom God loved better, the repentant sinner or the righteous. They usually decided on the righteous. Jesus differs radically.

## The Searching Woman

Next read **15:8-10**, the second parable on the theme of God's searching love and joy at the sinner's return. Jesus uses a woman as the symbol for God, something extremely unusual in Judaism. He refuses to be bound by cultural strictures that seek to devalue any person or group of people.

The woman has lost one of ten coins (*drachmas*), probably from her wedding headdress. The coins represent her dowry. All ten would be worth about ten days' wages. The amount is significant for her, but not great. It is the sentimental value that is important and the fact that the coins are hers. She sweeps carefully *until she finds it*. There is no question of her giving up. When it is found she, like the shepherd in the preceding parable and the father in the parable below, gathers the community to celebrate the occasion. The return of the lost is a reason for God's people to celebrate *(rejoice with me)* just as the company of heaven rejoices.

## The Lost Sons, Part 1

In **15:11-24** we probably have Jesus' most famous parable. The title "The Prodigal Son" is misleading, for there are two lost sons in this story. This double parable most fully defines what Jesus means by sin, repentance, grace, and joy. As with the two preceding parables, the Lost Sons speaks of God's joy at the return of the lost. Life in the kingdom of God is once more defined.

Again, this parable is informed by the culture. In verse 12 the younger son does something that is apparently not recorded in any ancient or modern Middle Eastern literature when he asks his father for his share of the inheritance. What he implies is, "Dad, I can't wait for you to die." A Palestinian patriarch would have been expected to disown a child who said such a thing. It is an unheard-of thing to say. But, says Jesus, the father gives the son what he wants, which is to be independent of his father–made possible by the father's money. This son has not broken the law but rather has radically broken his relationship with his father. He wishes his father were dead.

The younger son liquidates his assets and leaves his father's home with the cash. The *distant country* would be a Gentile land. He then loses everything in expensive living. The listeners would expect him to find the nearest Jewish community in order to get help since he is unwilling or unable to go home. But the son hires out to a Gentile pig farmer. Pigs were unclean animals in Judaism. This detail shows how far the son has sunk. He feels cut off not only from family but from his community's religion as well.

When he comes to his senses, he prepares a classic statement of Jewish repentance. In Judaism repentance took three steps: 1) to compensate for what has been lost; 2) to confess the sin publicly; 3) to prove sincerity by a period lived apart from the family. So the son plans for all three. 1) He will confess: *Father I have sinned against heaven and before you ...* 2) He will compensate his father for the loss: *... treat me like one of your hired hands;* and 3) He will live apart from the family for a time, since hired hands lived in the village, not at their employer's home. He believes that repaying his father the money he lost will square things, which only shows his youthful ignorance He does not even think about how he will repay the father's pain, shame, and sleepless nights of wondering if his son is dead. There is no way he can repay his father.

In first-century Jewish culture the son would also have worried about the "kesassa" ceremony, which is later documented in the Talmud and in other writings. In this ceremony, the father filled a large pot with burnt corn, beans, and raisins. Then he broke the pot outside in front of his door and proclaimed publicly, "My son is cut off from his people." This would act like the "shun" of the Pennsylvania Dutch, which removes a person from religious and social community ties. Out of respect for the father's wishes, no one in the village would then have anything to do with the son. He would not be spoken to. No one would give him a job. This ceremony would be carried out when a family member lost property to the Gentiles, as the younger son has done.

Before he reaches the village, all the son's fears evaporate. There is no kesassa ceremony. The father (who has apparently been watching every day for a glimpse of his lost son) runs through the village to greet his son. This would have been a great humiliation for the father. Older men never ran; it was considered shameful. The father's humiliating act diverts the hostility of the community from the boy. The son makes a statement of repentance worthy of a follower of Jesus: *Father, I have sinned against heaven and before you; I am no longer worthy to be called your son.*

There is no question of repaying the father or of a testing period. Instead the father reinstates the son into the family instantly with the signet ring and the robe. The banquet will reintroduce the son into the community. He is totally restored, having done absolutely nothing to earn it. He is restored to his father only because the father loves and accepts him. Note that the son's repentance does not make the father love him. The father has always loved him. The boy's repentance opened the way for him to see his father's love. The father's acceptance will make the son acceptable to the entire community. The reference to the banquet is, as always in Jesus' parables, a reference to life in the kingdom of God.

## The Lost Sons, Part 2

Continue on with **15:25-32**. The story of the second son, the older boy, makes this a double parable. Jesus introduces the older son at the very beginning of the story. It is interesting to note that when the younger son demands his share of the inheritance, the older son takes his, too. *He divided his property between them.* We would have expected the older son to refuse it.

The actions of this older son in the second half of the parable show what is in his heart. If you heard the sounds of a party coming from your house, you would almost certainly run in to see what the good news was. Not the older son. He seems suspicious and lacking in trust. He stops outside and asks what is going on. As the older son and a loving brother, we would expect him to have been worried about his little brother's fate. It becomes obvious that the news that his brother is alive is of no interest to him at all. Instead this grown man stands in the street, in full view of a courtyard full of guests, and pouts. He greatly insults his family by refusing to take his place and welcome guests into his family's home. Any Palestinian father would have been expected either to ignore the son (until the guests had left) or to punish him publicly in order to save face as patriarch of his family. This father does neither. Again he does the unthinkable, the shameful. He leaves his guests and goes out to beg his rude son publicly to come to the party. By so doing, the father saves the older son from being shunned by the village for his despicable behavior.

For the second time in the same day the father sacrifices himself for the sake of his sons. But whereas the younger son was deeply moved by his father's display of love, the older son further insults his father where the guests may hear. He does not address his father with a proper title and then shows what he thinks of their relationship. He feels like a slave doing his duty, not like a son acting as a partner in the work. *I have never disobeyed your command.* He has kept the Law, but he does not love the father. *My friends* denotes that his friends are not the friends of his family. He calls his brother *this son of yours.* Arabic scholars have seen in this speech the older son intentionally writing himself out of the family.

The father's response now must surely be to take a stick and drive the man off the property. That is what the guests and the hearers of the parable would have both expected and approved. But again, the father humiliates himself, sacrifices himself in order to save his child from himself. He makes a tender and loving speech to the older son using the Greek word that means "dear son." The father begs the son to be joyful and to come to the banquet.

In this parable sin is redefined not as the breaking of the Law *(I have never disobeyed your command),* but rather sin is the breaking of a relationship with God. Repentance is redefined as acknowledgment of one's inability to repay the debt. Salvation is simply the grace of a loving father toward his totally undeserving children. The father's willingness to give himself for them is great beyond imagination. So far from earning our way into the kingdom of God, the Father is begging us to come in. It is only our refusal to forgive others that keeps us out of the messianic banquet of joy.

The parable is open-ended. Will the older son drop his superior attitude, ask his father's forgiveness, throw his arms around his brother and join the party? Jesus leaves the question open because it is the Pharisees, the older brothers, those lost within the Law, who must finish the story. And beyond the Pharisees, it is for all who see themselves as religious to finish the story.

## FOR FURTHER STUDY AND REFLECTION

### Memory Bank

1. Luke 15:8-10, the Lost Coin

### Research

1. Use a Bible dictionary to find out more about Herod Antipas, the ruler who wanted to kill Jesus (Luke 13:31, 32).

### Reflection

1. In the *Resource Book* read again the discussion of 14:25-33. What does it mean to give up everything?

2. Does your congregation have a way of finding the "lost" of your community? How well do you rejoice when one of the lost comes into your church on a Sunday morning?

3. In the parable of the Lost Sons, one is lost while he keeps the Law, one while he does not. With which son do you have more in common?

4. Many people connect repentance with punishment–what the younger lost son anticipated. What does Jesus say is the result of repentance? What part does punishment play?

## SUMMARY

Jesus' journey to Jerusalem concludes with a variety of teaching themes. Two of the most prominent are the right use of wealth and the fate of the rich. The parables of the Dishonest Manager, The Rich Man and Lazarus, and encounters with the Rich Ruler and Zacchaeus all speak to these themes. Jesus also talks about the coming of the kingdom of God, discipleship in that kingdom, and his impending death. Two healings occur in this section: the ten lepers and the blind beggar.

## BASIC BIBLE REFERENCES

Luke 16:1-31
    17:1-37
    18:1-43
    19:1-27

## WORD LIST

conflation

# *10*

# *The Journey to Jerusalem Concludes*

## *Jesus and Possessions*

Possessions and the use of money are major themes in chapter 16. Luke may have reinterpreted Jesus' Parable of the Dishonest Manager as a teaching on money and thus included it here with other teachings on the same subject. But it is open to question as to whether the use of money was this parable's original point.

Read **16:1-9**. If the parable ends at verse 7, the point of the parable is not making use of *dishonest wealth*. Rather Jesus is telling his hearers that they should be taking action in their crisis situation even as the dishonest manager took action in his crisis situation. Jesus is saying, "If even a crook is smart enough to take the action necessary to save himself in time of crisis, why can't you?"

Certainly Jesus' hearers would have expected him to condemn the crook. Jesus surprises them with a commendation on his ability to meet a crisis. There is no indication here that Jesus was commending dishonesty, only the alertness to the gravity of his situation. Those who heed Jesus' warnings should be at least as shrewd as this crook.

This would be a strange parable to tell the disciples. The original audience would more likely have been unbelievers whom Jesus seeks to warn. Verse 9 is rather confusing. The meaning seems to be that disciples should use money in giving alms so that, as the dishonest manager was received into the homes of those who owed him a favor, so shall disciples be received into the kingdom because of their generosity. The verse does not have the "flavor" of other of Jesus' sayings, but a change of context may account for that. Luke has seen in the Parable of the Dishonest Manager a teaching about the use of money, but the broader reference is to the exercise of prudence.

Continue on to read **16:10-13**. These verses contain arguments from the lesser to the greater. If one is not careful in the little matters, in day-to-day honesty and righteousness, who will trust one with what is really important? The sayings seem to be independent of the main parable and may have been included here because they speak of integrity with the possessions of another. The truth of the saying should be obvious.

## Law and Kingdom

Now read **16:14-18**. In these verses Jesus condemns the religious leaders' misinterpretations of the Law. The Scriptures–the Law and the Prophets–were *in effect* until John announced the coming of Jesus; that is, they were the ruling revelation of God's will. Since then the gospel of the kingdom has been in effect. There are some new ways of doing business: no retribution, no returning of evil for evil, no equating of wealth with piety. Yet, says Jesus, the Scriptures have not been done away with. The gospel has shed its light on the Scriptures to reveal the proper interpretations. The Pharisees and scribes have been misinterpreting the Scriptures in order to justify the status quo. An example, as we will soon see, has been in their interpretation of what the Scriptures say about wealth.

And while Jesus is on the subject of misinterpreting the Law, he will straighten them out on another mistake they have made. In Jesus' day women could not divorce their husbands, but a man could divorce his wife simply by writing out a statement that he was divorcing her (See Matthew 5:31). He could then place her belongings, including the children, outside the house. If the woman had no father or brothers to take her in, her situation–and the children's–could rapidly become desperate. According to the way the religious leaders interpreted the Law, the husband was then free to marry the latest object of his affections. By interpreting the Law correctly Jesus calls a halt to this heartless misuse of women: he declares that any man who thinks he can get away with this is guilty of breaking one of the Ten Commandments. So a Scripture, which has been used so often against women, became Jesus' defense of women against an obscene misinterpretation of God's Law.

## The Rich Man and Lazarus

In **16:19-31** we have the only one of Jesus' parables to contain proper names, Lazarus and Abraham. The Egyptians had many stories about the dead returning with messages. The original one was known as "the Journey of Si-Osiris." It concludes with these words: "He who has been good on earth, will be blessed in the kingdom of the dead, and he who has been evil on earth, will suffer in the kingdom of the dead." The twist that Jesus gives the story is the important point. Details of the afterlife are not Jesus' concern; they are bits of popular conceptions in Jesus' day and cannot be taken as his picture of life after death. The Pharisees are Jesus' audience, they who had made fun of Jesus' statements about the love of money.

The rich man showers luxuries on himself every day. The beggar at the gates is of no concern to him. Lazarus (the name means "God helps") suffers from a skin disease as well as hunger. What *fell from the rich man's table* would be pieces of bread that the guests used to dip into the dish. They then wiped their fingers on them and threw them under the table.

Lazarus in the afterlife is seated next to Abraham, the father of the Hebrew faith. The rich man seems to consider Lazarus as his servant. He shows no remorse for the former sufferings of Lazarus that he could easily have relieved. Abraham addresses the rich man as *Child* (the same word the father used to the prodigal). He may be Abraham's child, but that is no guarantee of salvation. The great gulf is the finality of God's judgment.

The parable could have ended at verse 26. But Jesus is here responding to the Pharisees' derision of his sayings about money. Jesus has made love of God and love of money mutually exclusive. The Pharisees had biblical warrant for saying that they could love both. They interpreted such texts as Deuteronomy 28:1-14 as speaking to individuals, clearly stating that those who obey God will receive material and financial blessings. They believed that the Scriptures justified their wealth and their love of it, for it was God's own blessing. It is only a short mental hop to add a "therefore": therefore, the poor are those whom God has cursed.

The Parable of the Rich Man and Lazarus completely refutes such an interpretation of the Scriptures. The rich man is far from blessed in God's sight. Lazarus was under no curse. His pain came not from God, but from his own selfishness. Jesus is not refuting the Scriptures, he is refuting the Pharisees' incorrect interpretation of them.

*Moses and the prophets* is a reference to the Old Testament, which in Jesus' day consisted of the Law–which Moses was thought to have written–and the books written by or about the prophets. The Scriptures contain the truth that the rich man's brothers need to hear if only they will interpret them without self-interest. But if they find a way around hearing the Scriptures, they will find a way to discount any message they do not like, even if delivered by one back from the dead.

## The Duties of Discipleship

The sayings in **17:1-10** are not related to chapter 16. The audience has shifted back to the disciples. Four teachings on discipleship are fitted together. The *little ones* of verse 2b refer to disciples (see Mark 9:42a). The warning is to those who should be mature enough in their faith that they do not set a poor example for those who are new to the Christian community. Leaders especially must provide a good example for new members.

The term *another disciple* (Greek: "your brother") in verse 3 often has the meaning "fellow Christian" in the New Testament. This is particularly true in the letters. The disciple has an ethical obligation to rebuke a fellow Christian who has fallen into sin, but this rebuke is for the sake of repentance followed by forgiveness. Forgiveness that follows true repentance is absolutely mandatory in the fellowship. To forgive is not based on friendly feelings. Jesus commands forgiveness. It is hard work and needs prayer and the strength that comes from God.

The disciples beg for an increase in their faith. The Greek text of Jesus' response implies, "If you had faith, and you do …" Jesus, then, is telling the disciples that they have enough faith to do wonderful things.

The parable in verses 7-10, usually called "The Unprofitable Servant," is connected to this section by the theme of discipleship. The master owns the slave's time and energy. The slave can never reach a point where he can say, "I've done enough, anything more goes in my credit column." No one in the Christian community can ever reach the place where the community "owes" them. They have never done more than their share. We are servants of Christ. Our time and energy are his.

## The Ten Lepers

As you read **17:11-19**, note that Luke's order again relocates Jesus *between Samaria and Galilee.* This would be a likely place for contact with Samaritans. The story falls into two sections. In verses 11-14 we have a healing story in which those in need beg for Jesus' help, Jesus instructs them, they follow the instructions, and they are healed. In verse 14 Jesus assumes their healing, which is not yet in evidence. He instructs them to go show the priests that they are clean. The healing occurs as they obey.

In verses 15-19, the focus is on the salvation of the Samaritan. All the lepers were healed, even those who did not return to give thanks to Jesus. When Jesus tells the Samaritan in verse 19 *your faith has made you well,* the verb for "made well" is the same one that is used in 19:9-10 where it is translated "saved." All were made well in the sense of physical healing, but the grateful one was saved, for he acknowledged God's power in his life. The fact that the one who was saved was a foreigner and a religious heretic only brings home the point of how far those have strayed who should be close to God.

## Signs of the Kingdom

Now read **17:20-37**. This is a collection of Jesus' sayings concerning the coming of the kingdom and the parousia, the coming of the Son of Man. In verses 20-21 the Pharisees ask for a timetable for the kingdom (reign) of God. The coming reign of God was a popular concept. It was to be the time of which Isaiah spoke when peace and justice would reign and when death would no longer threaten (see Isaiah 11:1-9). Many tried to ascertain the time by interpreting signs–world events, natural phenomena, searching the Scriptures, and the like. Jesus warns against all such attempts. He says flatly that there will be no such observable signs. God's time is God's time. It is presumptuous to think that humans can predict it.

The translation of verse 21b has caused much confusion. The NRSV translates it, *For, in fact, the kingdom of God is among you.* Although the word translated "among" can also mean "within," there are reasons to prefer the former. Greek has different words for "you" singular and "you" plural. The word for "you" in this sentence is plural. The thought is not that there is some spark of God within each individual. Modern Western thought likes to think that way, but it is not biblical. Secondly, the "you" to whom Jesus is speaking are those who oppose Jesus and have not received the gospel message. It is not likely that Jesus would tell them that the kingdom of God was within them!

What is more likely is that Jesus is telling those who stand before him begging for signs that the ultimate sign of God's reign breaking into human society is Jesus himself. Here he stands, flesh and blood, inches away, and they want signs. Jesus has raised the dead, healed the ill, cured the insane, and they ask for a sign. God is already breaking into their lives and they are blind to it.

In verse 22 the audience shifts to the disciples. Here the subject is the parousia. In all four Gospels Jesus refers to himself as the Son of Man. That title is used in the Old Testament to mean a human being (see, for example, Ezekiel 2:1-3). In Old Testament apocalyptic writing it sometimes also refers to a heavenly figure who will be the future redeemer (see Daniel 7:13-14). Why or in what sense Jesus used the term of himself is open to question. It most often seems to be used as a substitute for "I." In the present verse it could be argued that Jesus is speaking of himself as the heavenly redeemer. Jesus tells the disciples that though they long for the parousia, they themselves will not see it.

In verse 23 Jesus repeats the warning that there will be no signs for so-called prophets to interpret. In verse 24 he assures his hearers that the coming of the Son of Man will be as obvious to all as lightning lighting up the whole sky. Verse 25 is a brief reference to Jesus' coming suffering in Jerusalem. Later he will elaborate on his death (18:31-33), which is bound up with the coming of the Son of Man.

The arrival of the Son of Man will be as sudden and unexpected as lightning. To make this point, Jesus refers to the unexpectedness of the flood in the Noah story (Genesis 7:6-24) and the unexpected destruction of Sodom (Genesis 18:20-33). The only time for preparation is in the life one lives day by day. Jesus' answer to the question *Where, Lord?* is, "You'll know when you see it." You only know where the body is when you see the vultures. Jesus is not giving times or places, and he does not expect his disciples to worry about them either.

## God's Vindication

Read **18:1-14**. Once again Luke has put contrasting parables back to back. There is more to the placement of the two parables here than the subject of prayer. The first parable concerns God's vindication of the righteous; the second concerns God's vindication of sinners.

The discussion in 17:20-37 centered on the coming of the kingdom and of the Son of Man. The Parable of the Widow and the Unjust Judge continues that theme. How long would it be before God vindicated his servants? The hope given in this parable must have been particularly important for the readers of Luke's day. They were beginning to see persecutions but not the return of the Lord (see 18:1). Once again, the argument in the parable is from the lesser to the greater. If even a rotten, corrupt judge can be made to do the right thing, how much more will a loving and just God be sure to do what is right for his servants? The parable ends at verse 5. Verses 6, 7, and 8a are a great assurance for the disciples. They must not give up their faith. God will act. But in verse 8b there is a warning as well: at the parousia, will the Son of Man find long-suffering faith?

The thrust of the Parable of the Pharisee and the Tax Collector is God's vindication of and mercy on sinners. The message contained here is at the heart of Christ's gospel: God is able and willing to save sinners, but the self-righteous reject God's salvation.

The Pharisee in the story is not an evil person. He is perfectly honest in all that he says. He has gone well beyond the demands of the Law. The Law only demanded a fast on the Day of Atonement, but Pharisees fasted every Monday and Thursday for the sins of the people. His tithing also was more than the Law required. His prayer is in the spirit of Psalms 17:3-5. He is, in the eyes of the people, a good man.

By contrast, the tax collector was considered to be the lowest sort of vermin: a traitor in his occupied land, a thief, an outcast from Judaism who did not deserve the name of Jew. He has no redeeming qualities.

Jesus' audience would certainly have expected the Pharisee to be justified. The belief was current that God did not save sinners. (So in John 9:31a a man says, *We know that God does not listen to sinners …*) Why, then, was the Pharisee not justified instead of the worthless tax collector? Luke provides the answer in his introduction to the parable. The Pharisees' problem was that they trusted in their good lives, not in God. The evidence of the Pharisees' lack of trust in God was their treatment of others: they despised them. True love of God issues in love of the neighbor.

Both prayers were answered. The tax collector received mercy for the asking. The Pharisee received nothing, for he asked God for nothing. The reversal theme plays itself out within this parable. The warning in verse 14 is not for Pharisees only but for all the so-called righteous who believe that their lives of good deeds will put God in their debt. (They should heed the words of the Parable of the Unprofitable Servant). This warning is often repeated by Jesus. There will be a final reversal of values in the fullness of the kingdom.

## Jesus and the Children

Now Read **18:15-17**. This passage is connected to the preceding ones by the theme of grace. It is God alone who justifies and blesses; our deeds earn us nothing. The children in this version are *infants*. They have done no good works, they have "earned" nothing. Just as parents love their infants simply because they are their children, so God loves people simply because they are God's, not because they are deserving. Jesus' pronouncement in verse 17 is not a call for disciples to be naive or childish. Rather, just as infants have no good works to present to their parents, so we must come before God with empty hands, not with a pharisaical list of good deeds.

## The Rich Ruler

The story of the Rich Ruler in **18:18-30** continues the theme of verse 14. This rich ruler (Matthew 19:20 says he was *young*) may be a synagogue ruler. He is certainly an observant Jew. But he, like the Pharisee in the above parable, is a kind of idolater. The Pharisee trusted in his goodness; the ruler trusts in his money. He cannot let go of his wealth and cling to Jesus. He sees his status, his comfort, and his safety as more important than God's will. He has grown accustomed to all that money can do for him. Having been lured deep into materialism, he cannot now envision life without wealth.

The rich ruler was already on the wrong track when he asked Jesus, *What must I do to inherit eternal life?* One does not have to "do" anything to gain an inheritance. He thinks in terms of earning eternal life.[1] He has, moreover, not kept the Law, for idolatry is banned in the Ten Commandments (Exodus 20:3).

Jesus' comment on the eye of the needle has nothing to do with a narrow passage which camels had to squeeze through. It is hyperbole. Jesus means that it simply cannot be done. The rich have too much to lose. Jesus' remarks stun the hearers. Salvation is impossible for any human to achieve, says Jesus. But it is not impossible for God to bestow it as a gift.

---

1 John's Gospel uses the term "eternal life" almost exclusively instead of and synonymous with "kingdom of God" or "kingdom of heaven".

Jesus' statement is reminiscent of the angel's response to Abraham and Sarah (Genesis 18:14) and likewise to Mary (Luke 1:37).

Peter speaks for all the disciples in reminding Jesus of what they have left for his sake. Jesus' reply about being given much more in the present age perhaps meant the gift of the fellowship of the Christian community, which is a foretaste of the kingdom. Jesus' followers will inherit as well the coming kingdom in all its fullness.

## Jesus Speaks About His Death

In the next section our attention is again turned toward Jerusalem as Jesus speaks for the third time about his death. Read **18:31-34**. Jesus implicates the Gentiles, that is, the Romans. The specific details about his passion may be an expansion made by the early Church after the fact. The disciples do not understand what Jesus is talking about because it is *hidden from them* by God. Luke makes a similar statement in 9:45. Understanding what the death and resurrection of Jesus mean does not come by observation but by revelation. It is only understood through the eyes of faith. After the resurrection Christ will give them understanding (24:27).

## Healing a Blind Beggar

Read **18:35-43**. Jesus is now close to Jerusalem, for Jericho is the last sizable town in the Jordan Valley before the ascent to the city begins. A crowd is following him. The crowd is aware of who Jesus is. Many of them are probably pilgrims making their way to the Holy City to celebrate Passover.

In verse 34 the disciples are spiritually blind. In verses 35-38 we encounter a blind man who sees spiritually, for he calls out, *Jesus, Son of David.* Son of David is a term used for the Messiah. In 1:32 Gabriel tells Mary, *He will be great, and will be called the Son of the Most High, and the Lord God will give to him the throne of his ancestor David.* Jesus will shortly dispute the use of the term (20:41-44), but for now he accepts it from the beggar.

Jesus does not assume that he knows what the man's problem is. Physical blindness may not have been the reason for his cry. Jesus restores the man's sight and pronounces the benediction: *Your faith has saved you.* TEV reads, "Your faith has made you well." The word for "saved" and "made well" is the same in Greek. It will be used again in 19:10.

## Zacchaeus

Turn to **19:1-10** now. The story of the salvation of a very poor man is followed by the story of the salvation of a very rich man. Zacchaeus also provides a contrast with the story of the religiously observant rich ruler. We meet Zacchaeus only in this Gospel. Luke says that Zacchaeus was a *chief tax collector.* Zacchaeus, then, is deeply implicated in the corrupt Roman tax system that kept so many of his own people in crushing poverty.

Luke does not tell us the inner workings of Zacchaeus' mind, but Zacchaeus is more than a little interested in seeing Jesus. Men of wealth did not climb trees in the ancient Near East. It would have been considered a very humiliating and foolish thing to do. Was he so lonely that he was willing to endure public humiliation merely to see a *friend of tax collectors and sinners* (7:34) pass by?

Jesus invites himself to dinner at Zacchaeus' house, a fact that sets the crowd grumbling with jealousy. They all wanted to rub elbows publicly with the celebrity. By the following week they will not be so eager to be seen with Jesus. They make the usual complaint against him.

Zacchaeus is apparently moved to a deep repentance by Jesus' willingness to sit at table with him as a friend. There is no record of Jesus' lecturing or shaming Zacchaeus. That Zacchaeus' repentance is genuine is seen by the fruit which it bears: love for his neighbors. Zacchaeus has borne the fruits of repentance which John the Baptizer demanded (3:10-14).

It should be noted that Zacchaeus goes far beyond the requirements of the Law in his restitution. He needed only to return the original amount plus twenty percent (Numbers 5:7). Zacchaeus first gives away half of all he owns. He then makes a fourfold restitution to those he has wronged. Zacchaeus has received the love of God; he now is able to give, not from the obligations of the Law, but from the Law of love. The Zacchaeus story is an example of Jesus' declaration, *What is impossible for mortals is possible for God* (18:27). Zacchaeus' salvation is lived out, not only in his inner heart, but in his family life, *this house,* and in his business and financial life as well. Repentance and salvation change every aspect of life.

## The Parable of the Ten Pounds

Now Read **19:11-27**. According to Luke Jesus tells this parable to clear up a misunderstanding: because they are nearing Jerusalem, some suppose that the kingdom of God is about to appear. What follows is, most likely, a conflation, the collapsing of two separate parables into one. Verses 12, 14, 15a, and 27 tell the story of an unpopular nobleman who goes abroad to receive kingly power, but is opposed by those at home, while verses 12 and 15-26 are the Parable of the Pounds.

Here the two stories are woven together. The story of the nobleman going abroad to receive power may have been developed from a historical incident. In 4 B.C. Archelaus, son of Herod the Great, went to Rome to receive the title of king after his father's death. But Archelaus was so hated by the Jews that a deputation of fifty men went to Rome to protest. Archelaus was not given the kingship, but he ruled Judea briefly. On his return from Rome he carried out a bloody revenge against his enemies.

There is a warning here for those who oppose the reign of God. Jesus is going away, but he will return with all the power of God. Jesus is in no way comparing himself to the sinful Archelaus, but he is using the incident to warn those who reject God's kingship that the coming of the Son of Man will be a dreadful day for them. Remember, too, that warnings are given in order to save those being warned. Jesus warns his enemies that to oppose God's kingdom is death and not life. Jesus would save his enemies if only they will receive the kingdom which his ministry brings.

The other story, the Parable of the Pounds, was originally told to warn the Pharisees and also the scribes, the custodians of the word of God. They have been entrusted with the riches of God's word, but they have been unfaithful, untrusting, and lazy servants. They should have been out in the world taking the risks of love and mercy and justice. But they have not even taken the simplest, beginning steps to increase God's word.

The readers of Luke's day would not have been concerned with the Pharisees and scribes, so the parable was reinterpreted to warn the disciples–the church–that they had been entrusted with God's gospel. God expects an increase on the investment. There will be an accounting. Had the church increased God's love and mercy and justice? Had Christ's disciples risked themselves out in the world by living the gospel? Faithful servants will have much, but those who refuse to trade with the word of God out in the world, even in the simplest way, will end up with nothing.

## FOR FURTHER STUDY AND DISCUSSION

### Memory Bank

1. Luke 16:10, 13. A reminder about how integrity and character are formed.

2. 17:10. A corrective for when we are tempted to list all we have done as earning a "place at the table."

### Research

1. Read the article on "steward" in a Bible dictionary or other resource. Then use a concordance to look at the ways Jesus uses the term.

### Reflection

1. On a world scale, the vast majority of westerners are very rich. According to Jesus, what are our responsibilities to the poor of the world?

2. In what way is your personal or family budget a statement of faith?

## SUMMARY

Jesus enters Jerusalem to the accolades of his disciples. He laments over the fate of the city and enters the Temple in order to make it a fit place for God's word. When the chief priests and lawyers question Jesus' authority, a heated discussion ensues. Jesus makes pronouncements about the destruction of Jerusalem and the Temple and also concerning the parousia. His teaching during this time includes the parables of the Tenants in the Vineyard and the Fig Tree.

## BASIC BIBLE REFERENCES

Luke 19:28-48
    20:1-47
    21:1-38
Zechariah 9:9-10

## WORD LIST

Sadducees
levirate marriage
apocalyptic

*11*

# *Jesus' Ministry in Jerusalem*

## *The Entry into Jerusalem*

Begin your study with **Luke 19:28-40**. The journey to the Holy City ends as Jesus enters the suburbs of Jerusalem. He sends disciples ahead of him into a nearby village to secure the colt upon which he will make his entrance into the city. He has given them a kind of password. Recall that Jesus made similar preparations at the beginning of the journey (9:52). He will do the same as he instructs the disciples to prepare the Passover meal (22:8-12).

The triumphal entrance has definite messianic overtones. A previously unused animal is appropriate for holy use. The details follow a prophetic pattern; read **Zechariah 9:9-10**, a messianic text exalting the work of "the prince of peace." Matthew and John quote the passage directly in their parallels to this story.

Jesus enters Jerusalem, not as one about to do battle, but as one who is already the victor, a symbolic action. A general or king subduing a city would enter decked out in armor and riding on a war horse. But a conqueror who was in control and to whom the city had already fallen would enter on a simple beast of burden; he would have no need of protection or a show of might. Luke mentions no palm branches, no hosannas or shouts of *Blessed is the coming kingdom of our ancestor David!* (Mark 11:10). These words and symbols had nationalistic overtones, something Luke apparently is attempting to play down.

Verse 38 is a quote from Psalm 118:26, a psalm praising God for victory. The shout is coupled with an echo of the words spoken by the heavenly host at Jesus' birth (Luke 2:14). The designation of *king* is combined with the coming of peace; this king is the one bringing in God's reign of peace. The whole episode takes on the flavor of an acted-out parable. The man entering the gates of the city on a colt is, in fact, the victorious God coming to begin his reign.

Are the Pharisees angry with Jesus (verse 39), or are they concerned for his safety and perhaps their own? Some Pharisees had tried to warn Jesus before when it looked as if he were headed for trouble with the rulers (13:31). Luke does not tell us their motivation. Jesus' reply means that there is no stopping the truth–it will finally be heard. Jesus is also saying that the shouts of the crowd of disciples have been correct.

## Weeping Over Jerusalem

Now read **19:41-44**. In 13:31-35 Jesus lamented over Jerusalem. Here the lament continues. The leaders of Israel, in Luke's view, had rejected God's offer of life and had pinned their hopes on political and military solutions instead. A little more than three decades after Jesus' lament Israel would attempt to survive by going to war with Rome. Jerusalem was destroyed in A.D. 70 and the Temple was demolished. It has not been rebuilt to this day. The description of the siege of Jerusalem in verses 43-44 is much as it actually happened. Jesus makes a definite connection between the destruction of Jerusalem and the Temple and the nation's rejection of himself.

## The Temple

Move on to **19:45-48**. The Temple is very prominent in Luke's Gospel. Zechariah is in the Temple when he receives word of the Messiah's impending birth (1:11-17). Jesus is dedicated in the Temple, and there Simeon acclaims him to be the Messiah (2:22-38). At age twelve, when Jesus is found in the Temple, he tells his parents *I must be in my Father's house* (2:49). Here as Jesus arrives at last in the Holy City his first act is to go into the Temple. The Temple will be Jesus' center for teaching while he is in Jerusalem. Following the resurrection in Matthew and Mark, Christ instructs the disciples to go to Galilee to meet him. But in Luke they last see Jesus in the suburbs of Jerusalem, and Luke ends the Gospel by indicating that the disciples spent all their time in the Temple (24:53). This Temple activity is significant for Luke, symbolizing that Jesus is the fulfillment of all God's promises to Israel.

There was only one Temple and it was regarded as the holiest spot in Israel. Every observant Jew wanted to celebrate at least one Passover in Jerusalem in order to offer sacrifice in the Temple. Jesus arrived in Jerusalem during Passover week. This meant that there would be thousands upon thousands of pilgrims in the city, all desiring to go to the Temple.

*Those who were selling* would be present for two reasons. First, they would be selling unblemished sacrificial animals to pilgrims who had traveled many miles. Cages of pigeons and pens of sheep and goats would be set up for this purpose. Second, the payment of the Temple tax could not be made with the Roman denarius since it was engraved with the image of Caesar. The money needed to be changed to the Hebrew drachma. Jesus indicates that the merchants were cheating the people, probably by charging exorbitant prices.

Jesus' action of ridding the Temple precincts of these merchants amounts to a purging or cleansing of the Temple. But as in his parable of the Return of the Evil Spirit (11:24-26), Jesus does not leave God's house clean and empty. He proceeds to teach every day in the Temple, filling it with God's truth. The prophet Malachi wrote about a cleansing of the Temple; see 3:1-4. Jesus' actions echo this passage. Jesus' cleansing of the Temple and his use of it as a center for teaching enrages his enemies.

A new set of adversaries has come into the picture: the chief priests and the *leaders of the people*. This phrase may refer to some of the members of the Sanhedrin (see Part 3). The scribes and Pharisees' debates with Jesus were over points of the Law and its interpretation. In using the Temple for his teaching Jesus invades the turf of the chief priests, since they are the professional clergy who work there every day. They must bottle up their jealousy and anger, for the crowds are definitely with Jesus.

## Challenging Jesus' Authority

The chief priests, scribes, and elders ("the leaders of the people") finally summon the courage to confront Jesus. Read **20:1-8**. On the one hand, they have a perfect right to do so. Any religion needs to have lines of accountability for its leaders and spokespersons. Jesus has not come up through the system; he is a layman who has been granted no status, except by the common people who flock to him. Had the leaders' reason for questioning

Jesus been legitimate, however, Jesus would have answered their question. But it has been obvious for some time that these leaders have no intention of keeping an open mind. The reason for the question is simply to accuse Jesus and denounce him before the people. They prove this to be the case by the way they answer Jesus' question to them. They do not huddle to discuss an honest answer, but to discuss what is expedient to say in front of the crowd. Neither then, would they be interested in Jesus' honest answer. Jesus refuses to play their game. Had they come to Jesus to hear sincerely what he had to say, he would have taught them as he did the crowds.

## *The Parable of the Wicked Tenants*

Continue reading through **20:9-19**. Jesus resumes teaching the crowds, but he is really addressing the chief priests, scribes, and elders who are still there. Jesus speaks to them indirectly as they overhear what he is saying. It is only as Jesus is well into his story that they realize they are its subject. This parable is more of an allegory dealing with real events that have been veiled in story form.

The vineyard had long been symbolic of Israel (see Isaiah 5:1-7; Ezekiel 15:1-6) and of the effort God expended on the people. The tenants may mean all those who had authority in Judaism throughout the centuries. The tenants in question are those at the end of this long line: the chief priests, scribes and elders who are, even now, listening to this parable. The slaves of the owner would be the prophets, up to and including John the Baptizer. The *beloved son* is Jesus.

If the hearers perceive that Jesus is the beloved son and that the owner of the vineyard is God, they will have their answer to the question about Jesus' authority. It is the way in which people (and the nation) respond to Jesus that determines their status with God. The destruction of the tenants (leaders) means the destruction of the nation. Jerusalem, the Temple, and the nation had fallen in 587 B.C. when Israel had rejected the message of God's prophets. Here Jesus warns that such a sequence of events is about to be repeated. This message causes the crowds to utter a shocked, *Heaven forbid!* As the people protest, Jesus reminds them of Psalms 118:22. He then alludes to Isaiah 8:14-15. Beyond the fall of Jerusalem, Jesus is predicting that God's Word will now be in the hands of others; God will move beyond the walls of Israel into the whole world, the world of the Gentiles.

Luke does not include this parable simply as a way of gloating over what happened to Jesus' enemies. It serves as a warning that any leader of the church, any proclaimer of the Word, is a tenant only. He or she is accountable to God for every word and action. The chief priests, scribes, and elders have had a clear warning from Jesus to turn away from the path to destruction. But they are deaf as well as blind. *They wanted to lay hands on him at that very hour, but they feared the people* (20:19).

## A Question About Taxes

Read **20:20-26**. The leaders now throw their campaign against Jesus into high gear. Unable to trap him with their questions, they now send hired spies. They have already decided that Jesus must die, for their plan is to hand him over to *the jurisdiction and authority of the governor.* The Romans did not allow Israel to carry out capital punishment. In order to have Jesus legally killed, his enemies must be able to get a conviction on a crime against the Roman Empire. Advising the people not to pay taxes to Rome would certainly be cause enough.

The taxes paid to Rome were a very sore point with the people of Israel, who resented paying tribute to Gentile pagans. Some had called the paying of such taxes treason. If Jesus answers that the taxes should be paid, the crowd is sure to turn against him. Then the way will be clear for Jesus' enemies to do whatever they want with him. If Jesus answers that the Roman taxes should not be paid, his enemies will have grounds for bringing him before the Roman authorities.

Jesus' pronouncement in verse 25 is more than a clever balancing act. He never denounced the power of governments to make laws and to govern. They have legitimate authority. But what is due to God always supersedes what is due to the state. The coin which Jesus held had Caesar's image on it and so may well be due to Caesar; the people to whom Jesus spoke knew that they were made in God's image (Genesis 1:26a) and therefore belonged heart and soul to God. This shuts the mouths of the hired spies. A new group of questioners will now take their place.

## A Question About Resurrection

Now read **20:27-40**. This will be the final question that Jesus' adversaries put to him. Luke does not indicate that the question is a trap. It is asked by the Sadducees, one of the many parties in Judaism. They were men from the priestly class, aristocratic and often wealthy, who had a vested interest in keeping things as they were. Because they were conservative, they tried to appease the Romans by going along with them.

The Sadducees held only the Pentateuch as authoritative. The Pharisees accepted, in addition, the Prophets, most of the Writings, and oral tradition. This created conflicts between the Sadducees and the Pharisees about many beliefs including the general resurrection at the last day. The Pharisees believed in it; since it is not mentioned in the Pentateuch, the Sadducees did not.[1] The resurrection was one of many areas of agreement that Jesus had with the Pharisees. Belief in a resurrection of the dead had been current among the Pharisees and many of the people for years. Warrant for it could be found in the oral tradition. For a statement of the common pharisaical belief of the day see Martha's response to Jesus in John 11:23-24.

The question posed by the Sadducees is based on the concept of levirate marriage, a law contained in Deuteronomy 25:5-10. In early Jewish thought a person lived on after death by having a son to bear the name and tell the story. It was the duty of the brother of a man who died childless to have a son by the man's widow. That child would be considered the child of the deceased. The Sadducees come to Jesus with a question about how such a system would work out in the so-called afterlife–in which they did not believe.

Jesus answers their question in two parts. First, the Sadducees are trying to compare apples and oranges, life in this age and life in the age to come. In the life to come there is no death, hence no need for marriage (the propagation of life) and no need for levirate marriage. Secondly, Jesus gives evidence of the resurrection from the Sadducees' own Scriptures (Exodus 3:6). Since God is God of the living and the God of Abraham, Isaac, and Jacob, those patriarchs must be alive to God. This may sound to us like odd reasoning, but it is very much the style in which the rabbis debated. Since Jesus has argued the Pharisees' case for them, some of their scribes congratulate Jesus. Jesus has silenced the Sadducees. He leaves all the listeners without the courage to ask more questions.

---

1  In Acts Paul gets himself out of a tight spot by playing "Let's You and Him Fight" with the Pharisees and Sadducees on the subject of the resurrection (23:6-10).

## Jesus Asks a Question

In the ongoing debate between Jesus and his adversaries it is Jesus who asks the last question. He asks who and what the Messiah is. Read **20:41-44**. Jesus has been identified as the son of David three times in Luke (1:32, 69; 3:31). He did not contradict the blind beggar in 18:35-43 who called him *Son of David.* Jesus is a son of David in the sense of being a biological descendant. But if the designation is given to him in order to say that he is like David, that is, a military hero who will return Israel to its former political importance, the designation is misleading. Over the years the people had built up an understanding of who and what the Messiah would be. The definition closely resembled David, who reigned one thousand years before the birth of Jesus. Jesus redefines the meaning of the Messiah. The Messiah that God has actually sent is not like David. Jesus has come not to battle Israel's political enemies but the enemy that is their own rebelliousness before God. His reign as king will bring not political superiority for Israel, but God's sovereignty over all the earth. Jesus uses the opening verse of Psalm 110 to argue that David, who was assumed to have written the Psalm, calls God's Messiah David's Lord, not his son. What God is accomplishing in Jesus is a new thing; it cannot be compared to any past person or event.

## Jesus Denounces the Scribes

Now read **20:45-47**. The audience is the disciples, but the crowds overhear what Jesus says. The disciples of Jesus are never to become the pompous, self-important kind of persons that too many of the scribes have become. God gave the scribes the vital duty of bringing people to God by teaching them God's word. But they had corrupted the task until it became an opportunity to make themselves important in the eyes of the people. They therefore both failed to lead the people to God, and usurped God's place. Jesus may be concerned that the disciples, who will shortly be in charge of his earthly fellowship, may also distort their duty into privilege.

The scribes show their self-centeredness in many ways: in their dress, by the way they enjoy the bowing and scraping of the crowds, reserved seats at worship, and head tables at social functions. These are behaviors Jesus' disciples must never covet or revel in.

Jesus accuses the scribes of devouring widows' houses. Scribes, because they were lawyers, would sometimes advise widows on legal and financial questions. They were often guardians of a deceased husband's will. This presented opportunities to cheat widows, to mismanage their estates, and to bring them to financial ruin. Jesus denounces this hypocrisy.

## *Jesus Exalts a Widow*

Continue on with **21:1-4**. The widow's unselfish devotion to God is set in contrast to the scribes' selfish devotion to themselves. The scribes honor themselves before the people instead of honoring God. The widow, whom the scribes would be only too willing to cheat, honors God with her act. In making her offering to God she has given all. For tomorrow, she must now trust God not her savings. Again, the reign of God turns the world's values upside down. Those who are great in the world are not necessarily great in the kingdom. The scribes desire the praise of people; this woman is praised by the Son of God.

## *Apocalyptic*

Read **21:5-38**. In order to deal with these verses a specific type of literature, "apocalyptic," needs to be explored. In apocalyptic the author purports to have received a message, usually delivered by angels, about the final cataclysmic end of time and the imminent coming of a new age where God rules. This was a type of writing well-known in Jesus' day. It dates back to the Old Testament. The books of Daniel, Ezekiel, and Zechariah all contain apocalyptic. The book of Revelation in the New Testament is thoroughgoing apocalyptic.

The word "apocalypse" means "revelation." Apocalyptic literature is most popular during times when a nation or people is under extreme stress. To the people who are suffering it looks as if things are so bad, evil has such an upper hand, that the only way out is for God to come forcefully and overwhelm the current situation. This amazing literature encourages the community to keep faith with God even in the worst of circumstances.

It is common for a piece of apocalyptic literature to describe the destruction of the earth and the universe, the judgment of God's enemies (always those who are oppressing the writer's audience), and the vindication of God's people. Apocalyptic is filled with signs and symbols. Because it is written during times of crisis, the historical situation is usually reflected in the text.

## The End of the Temple

In verses 5-11 a discussion of the beauty of the Temple in Jerusalem prompts Jesus to predict its destruction. As we have seen, that destruction came with the fall of Jerusalem and the overthrow of Israel by the Romans in A.D. 70. The prediction itself is not cast in apocalyptic form; it is not stated in symbolic language. His speech is the kind of warning the prophets of the Old Testament so often gave to the people.

In verses 7-9 Jesus repeats his warnings against looking for signs. He denounces those who would lead people astray by pretending to be able to predict the future. In 17:20, when Jesus denounced those who put their trust in signs, he was referring to the coming of the kingdom of God. Here Jesus warns about looking for signs of the fall of Jerusalem.

*Earthquakes, plagues,* and *dreadful portents and great signs from heaven* are apocalyptic imagery. It would be almost impossible to know whether Jesus connected the destruction of Israel to the end of time or whether the Gospel writers, living in the midst of terrifying times, combined Jesus' words about Jerusalem and the Temple with sayings about the end of time.

## The Persecution of the Disciples

In verses 12-19 we have a description of what the disciples of Jesus can expect to suffer. In times of political stress and danger, those who deviate from the majority in any way are seen as a threat. The nation tries to close ranks; hence those who do not go along are frequently persecuted. This is what happened to the early Christians. Jesus promises his followers that they will be given the right words to say when they are made to defend themselves. This knowledge will be given by the Holy Spirit. Verse 18 probably does not mean that the disciples will not die. Disciples had already been murdered by the time Luke wrote. Instead it may have the sense of 12:4-5, *Do not fear those who kill the body, and after that can do nothing more … fear him who, after he has killed, has authority to cast into hell.* The loyal disciple's death cannot destroy the disciple. This persecution will begin before Jerusalem is destroyed. The disciples are not to lose heart; God has not forgotten them.

## Jesus Tells of the Fall of Jerusalem

In verses 20-24 Jesus gives a short but vivid picture of the destruction of Israel's capital city and site of its holiest shrine. The fall of the capital means the fall of the nation. Jesus speaks of the *times of the Gentiles.* This may refer to the time of the mission to the world beyond Israel's borders. It is this mission that is the subject of Acts. The language here does not speak of a cataclysmic end of time–it is not apocalyptic. It contains no symbols. This is simply a description of what could be a historical event.

## The Coming of the Son of Man

In verses 25-28, however, the language has shifted to apocalyptic and concerns the end of time. Verse 25 speaks of astronomical signs, a very common apocalyptic theme. By placing these verses here, sayings about final things and about Jerusalem's fall may have been combined. The coming of the Son of Man in glory affects the entire universe. But Jesus does not speak of a cataclysmic end of time and the destruction of the present world. The coming of the Son of Man will change life dramatically, but there is no support in these words for thoroughgoing classical apocalyptic.

## The Fig Tree

The parabolic saying in verses 29-33 is about recognizing the coming of the kingdom. Because of the powerful things that are happening, it will be as obvious as seeing summer's approach in the leafing of the trees. It will not take a prophet to know that God's reign is coming. Does verse 32 refer to the coming of the kingdom or the fall of Jerusalem? The people of Luke's generation did not see the kingdom come in all its fullness. They did see Jerusalem destroyed about forty years after Jesus' prediction.

## Watch!

The words in verses 34-36 sound very much like some of Jesus' crisis parables (see for example 12:35-48, 54-56). Again, the advent of the kingdom is coming *upon all who live on the face of the whole earth.* The theme of universality, of moving beyond the boundaries of Israel, is sounded again and again in this Gospel. All will *stand before the Son of Man.* Verses 37-38 are a transition. Jesus' discourses are at an end. From now on everything that happens and everything that Jesus says will be in the context of his imminent death.

# FOR FURTHER STUDY AND DISCUSSION

### Memory Bank

1. Luke 21:3, 4. Jesus' commendation of the poor widow.

### Research

1. Read Deuteronomy 25:5-10, the connection between levirate marriage and how a man "lived on" after death. Read about "Eternal Life" in a Bible dictionary or another reference work. What interpretations for Jesus' defeat of death does the New Testament give?

2. In a reference book read about the Third Temple, the one Jesus knew. Imagine the variety of religious and national feelings the Temple must have held for Jews contemporary with Jesus. What must it have been like to see pagan troops destroy it?

### Reflection

1. Imagine yourself a first century Jew in Israel. How would you feel about Jesus' cleansing of the Temple? About Jesus' words concerning the destruction of the Temple?

2. How can you reconcile Jesus' love for the Temple with his pronouncement of its doom?

## SUMMARY

Jesus' enemies find a way to destroy him when one of the Twelve offers them an occasion. Jesus makes plans to celebrate Passover with his disciples. During the Passover meal he institutes the Lord's Supper. He begins his farewell speech to the disciples, but in the midst of it the Twelve argue about which of them is greater. Judas' treachery and Peter's denial are predicted. Then Jesus goes to the Mount of Olives to pray.

## BASIC BIBLE REFERENCES

Luke 22:1-46
1 Corinthians 11:23-26;
    15:3-7
Exodus 12:1-20
Matthew 26:20-30; 36-46
Mark 14:17-26, 32-42
John 6:48-58; 13:21-30;
    18:1-2

## WORD LIST

Passover
Maundy Thursday
Seder
kosher
messianic banquet
Satan

# *The Passion Narrative (1)*

## *The Narratives of Holy Week*

As we have seen in Part 1, the Gospels are their own unique category of writing and not biographies. Nowhere is this more evident than in the sections on the death and resurrection of Jesus. Of Luke's twenty-four chapters, four are devoted to the last six days of Jesus' life. It is much the same in Mark and Matthew. John's Gospel devotes nine of its twenty-one chapters to that one last week which the church calls Holy Week.

These final chapters, then, are to be considered the heart of the Gospel, the focus toward which all else is directed. Luke has used his travel narrative as a way of reminding us that everything Jesus does and says is moving him steadily toward that final confrontation in Jerusalem. It is here that the powers of death are to be met and defeated.

The early church was built around the death and resurrection of Jesus. Before any of the Gospels had been written, the Christian community broke bread and shared the cup to celebrate the passion, as Jesus had commanded them. One of the earliest affirmations of Christian faith in the New Testament is found in Paul's first letter to Corinth; read **1 Corinthians 15:3-7.**[1] That affirmation is based entirely on Jesus' death and resurrection.

---

1   Remember that most of the Pauline letters predate the writing of the Gospels.

No matter what else we know about Jesus, it is as Paul says: *If Christ has not been raised, your faith is futile and you are still in your sins* (1 Corinthians 15:17).

## Jesus' Enemies Plot His Death

Read **Luke 22:1-6**. Up to this point Jesus' enemies have been stymied by the adoring crowds whose presence protects him from attack or arrest. Judas, who has not been mentioned since 6:16, enters the picture. He can do what Jesus' enemies–here identified as the chief priests and scribes–cannot do. Judas can supply information about where and when Jesus can be found without the crowds.

Why did Judas betray his own teacher? The question cannot be answered, although many have tried. Luke says that *Satan entered into Judas.* But we will shortly see that the entering of evil desires into Judas does not absolve him from responsibility. *For the Son of Man is going as it has been determined, but woe to that one by whom he is betrayed* (22:22). Something in Judas allowed evil to enter. It is not possible to know what that something was.

## Jesus Prepares to Celebrate Life

As you will see in **22:7-13**, Luke does not distinguish between Passover itself and the festival of Unleavened Bread. Unleavened Bread is a seven-day festival emphasizing the Exodus from Egypt. "Passover" literally refers to the death of the Egyptian firstborn, but usually it was used to designate the entire celebration. The Passover meal begins the festival. This is a joyful time in Judaism, for it is based on the Hebrew people's first encounter with God. They learn who God is as they are saved from slavery in Egypt and from death.

Review the story of the first Passover in **Exodus 12:1-20**. The death of the firstborn of the Egyptians was God's final plague. The Jews had been instructed to smear the blood of a lamb on their door posts so the destruction of the firstborn would "pass over them." The people were quite literally saved by the blood of the lamb.

In Luke 22:8-12 Jesus instructs Peter and John to prepare the Passover meal. These two disciples often constitute a pair and continue to do so in the book of Acts (3:1-4:22; 8:14-25). As on previous occasions, Jesus gives instructions for finding the people who are needed. A man carrying a water jar would be unusual; hauling water was women's work. This appears to be a prearranged signal; a password is given.

The preparation would consist of purchasing the food: bread, wine, herbs, the condiments necessary for a Passover meal, and a lamb that had been approved by a priest and slain in kosher fashion. To be considered kosher the animal must have its throat slit in order to allow the blood to drain from the body. The Jews did not eat meat with the blood in it (*strangled,* see Acts 15:29) because they believed that the life was in the blood (see Genesis 9:4).

## *The Lord's Supper*

Four places in the New Testament describe the institution of the Lord's Supper: Read **Matthew 26:20-30**; **Mark 14:17-26**; **Luke 22:14-20,** and **1 Corinthians 11:23-26**.[2] Three other names are commonly used for the Lord's Supper: Last Supper (used mainly during Holy Week observances), Holy Communion, and Eucharist (from a Greek root that means "thanksgiving"). All refer to the same meal. In liturgical churches the institution of the Lord's Supper is observed on the Thursday evening of Holy Week. This day is alternately called Holy Thursday or Maundy Thursday. "Maundy" is from a Latin root meaning "command" (from which also comes the English "mandate"). On this night Jesus commanded his followers to observe this meal in remembrance of him. In John's Gospel the *new commandment* (13:34) is given on this night.

The final meal in John's Gospel contains no description of the institution of the Lord's Supper. Read **John 13:21-30**. Here the footwashing is described instead. Now Read **John 6:48-58**. These words of Jesus would surely have been interpreted by the early church as referring to the Lord's Supper. John does not give the setting but instead marks the theological importance of the event.

## *Luke's Account of the Supper*

Read again Luke 22:14-20. The disciples who are gathered for this meal are the *apostles,* presumably the Twelve. The dinner is the Passover meal or Seder. At this meal the story of the Exodus was read and symbolic foods reminded the celebrants of their slavery and of God's deliverance. Jesus will not celebrate it again until it is *fulfilled in the kingdom of God.*

---

2    Throughout the sessions dealing with the passion and resurrection narratives (parts 12, 13, 14) we will look at parallel texts in the other three Gospels. The records do not match in a number of details, which is evidence of reliable witness. They have not been forced to agree.

He at once predicts that he will not live to see another earthly Passover, and emphasizes the eschatological meaning of this meal. Passover will receive its full meaning when in the kingdom all God's people are free from their bondage to sin. Jesus makes much the same statement with the cup of wine. Traditionally, during the Seder Psalm 118 was sung. It looks forward to an eschatological, perhaps even messianic, deliverance: *Blessed is the one who comes in the name of the Lord* (118:26). The next Passover that Jesus observes will be the eschatological messianic banquet.

Note that in Luke Jesus offers two cups of wine. Three and perhaps four cups of wine were usually offered at the Passover meal. Jesus, as the host, begins the meal with the first cup of wine and then comments on the finality of this earthly meal for himself. The cup in verse 20 is the cup given after supper, *the cup of blessing*. Paul calls it by this name in 1 Corinthians 10:16.

In verses 19-20 Jesus interprets the meaning of his death in terms of a sacrifice. The sacrifice of the Passover lamb was to seal the covenant between God and the people. In Luke it is not a sin offering; Jesus' blood will seal a new covenant saving God's people and freeing them for eternal life. This is one of the basic themes in the New Testament book of Hebrews; see for example, Hebrews 10. Several other places in the New Testament, however, interpret the blood of Jesus as an offering for sin. The Lord's Supper can only be fully understood in the context of its Jewish setting as a Seder. Luke again reminds us that Jesus, and the Christian faith, cannot be divorced from Judaism and the Old Testament.

Of the Gospels, only Luke includes the words *Do this in remembrance of me*. These words are also found in 1 Corinthians 11:24b (the earliest written record). The eating and drinking bind the disciples not only in a covenant with God, but with each other. In the Lord's Supper Jesus has formed a new community in his blood. This idea is expanded in Ephesians, where the writer speaks about the unity in Christ that breaks the barriers of race: *But now in Christ Jesus you who once were far off have been brought near by the blood of Christ. For he is our peace; in his flesh he has made both groups into one ....* (2:13-14a). Similarly, it is when the fledgling Christians of Corinth ignore the fellowship aspect of Holy Communion that Paul reminds them of Jesus' words of institution (see 1 Corinthians 11:17-22). The *you* in Luke 22:14-20 is plural. Christ's sacrifice and salvation are offered in and for the community.

## Betrayal Predicted

Now read **22:21-22**. Sharing in the sacrament is no guarantee of faithfulness. Luke is the only writer who puts Jesus' words about betrayal after the institution of the Lord's Supper. Judas has participated with the others. He is offered forgiveness and a place in the community even after he has decided to betray Jesus. Judas therefore betrays not only his master, but the community created in Jesus' blood.

## The Greatest

Continue with **22:23-30**. Only Luke places this dispute at the Last Supper. The controversy grows out of the disciples' discussion about which of them could betray Jesus. Their argument puts them on the verge of betraying Jesus and the faith community by giving first place to their pride instead of to God. These verses warn the whole church and especially those in leadership positions concerning the constant threat of betrayal of the Lord by the temptations that authority brings. The warning against trying to be important by exercising power over others in the Christian community is the same warning that Jesus communicates with the footwashing in John's Gospel (13:12-17). Here Jesus again sounds the theme of the reversal of values in the kingdom.

Jesus tells the disciples that their place in God's kingdom and at Christ's table at the messianic banquet is assured because he gives it to them. They have stood by him in his trials. The promise that the disciples will judge the twelve tribes of Israel is eschatological language. Again this is that reversal of fortune which has been a theme throughout Luke's Gospel. It does not mean that Gentiles will judge Jews (the people to whom Jesus is speaking are Jews) or that the church will be allowed to pass judgment on the synagogue. The word "judging" here may carry the Old Testament meaning of "ruling."

## Peter's Denial Predicted

In **22:31-34** we see that it was not only Judas who was tempted to betray Jesus (recall that the Hebrew word *satan* means "adversary, tempter"). *All of you* correctly translates the "you" of verse 31. The "you" in verse 32, however, is singular. Jesus has prayed for Peter not to fall. He will seriously waver but will turn back in order to lead the others out of their cowardice and again to discipleship. Peter's shocked response to Jesus is moving. Peter has begun to realize how serious the situation is: *I am ready to go with you to prison and to* *death!* He really wants to be that strong. But Jesus knows that when Peter's own life is on the line, when it looks as though Jesus has lost, Peter will deny him to save his own skin. This, too, constitutes a betrayal. Jesus' warning to Peter is given to help him live through the guilt and shame he will shortly suffer. Jesus has also assured this betrayer that forgiveness and a new start are possible.

## Swords

Jesus now makes an attempt to explain to all the disciples what they are about to face. Read **22:35-38**. He reminds them of the first time that they had to face the world without him, when he sent them out on preaching missions (9:1-6 and 10:1-12, 17-20). Then they had come back rejoicing and saying ... *even the demons submit to us*. It will not be like that now. Jesus, speaking symbolically, tells them that the situation into which they are about to be thrust is the kind where people want all the protection they can get, even to the point of selling their clothes in order to lay hands on a weapon to protect themselves. The disciples understand Jesus to be speaking literally and reveal that they have already begun to arm themselves. Jesus' reply has the sense of "enough of that." He will again repudiate the disciples' desire to defend him with violence (22:51).

Why are things about to go so terribly wrong for Jesus and his disciples? To provide a perspective on the situation Jesus quotes part of Isaiah 53:12. The entire verse reads:

> Therefore I will allot him a portion with the great,
> and he shall divide the spoil with the strong;
> because he poured out himself to death,
> and was numbered with the transgressors;
> yet he bore the sin of many,
> and made intercession for the transgressors.

Jesus looked to Isaiah, and especially passages such as this, as the model for his ministry. Now he sees the inevitable outcome of following God's way in a sinful world.

## On the Mount of Olives

Now read **Luke 22:39-46**. (Parallels are in **Matthew 26:36-46, Mark 14:32-42,** and **John 18:1-2**. It becomes evident very quickly that there are several differences in Luke's account when compared with the other Gospels. First, Luke's version is noticeably shorter than the others. What is missing in Luke is any description of Jesus' agony, upset, and pain. If we exclude verses 43-44, which will be discussed separately, there is no description at all in Luke of Jesus as being *grieved, agitated,* or *distressed* (Matthew's and Mark's words). Jesus simply goes to the Mount of Olives *as was his custom,* instructs the disciples to pray, and then prays himself. He does not pray three separate times, but once. And only once does he find the disciples asleep.

Notice that in Luke Jesus does not throw himself on the ground as in Matthew and Mark, but rather *he withdrew from them about a stone's throw, knelt down, and prayed.* Jesus is controlled and resolved. Why does Luke omit all references to Jesus' emotions? It may be that the people to whom Luke is writing, Gentiles versed in Judaism, would not understand anguish and grief on Jesus' part. Famous stoic philosophers in the Greek and Roman cultures had written centuries before Jesus that emotions such as sorrow were irrational, sinful, and the mark of one out of control. Certainly Luke does not want his readers to think of Jesus that way.

Only John goes further than Luke in eliminating any show of self-concern on Jesus' part; John eliminates the prayer altogether. Luke will not go that far. The prayer life of Jesus is one of Luke's major themes. He has shown us Jesus at prayer during all the crucial times of his life; here more than any other time Jesus will certainly pray.

Jesus not only prays but also instructs his disciples to do the same: *Pray that you may not come into the time of trial.* "Trial" is the same word that was used in the Lord's Prayer (see Part 7). To enter into a time of trial would be to succumb to the temptation to cut and run when the going gets tough, to deny God in order to save oneself. This is indeed the very real danger the disciples face. It is not simply a danger of the moment; there are eschatological implications: *but whoever denies me before others will be denied before the angels of God* (12:9). Jesus knows that the disciples will falter in this frightening time, but they must not fall. This was a prayer that Luke's readers needed to pray, for they were beginning to experience persecutions.

## *Jesus Prays*

The content of Jesus' prayer is given in one verse. Jesus wants the cup of suffering to be removed. He is asking God to change the plan. There are many precedents in the Old

Testament where God is asked, if it is acceptable, to do this. (See, for example, Exodus 32:10-14). Jesus, who loved life and the people, does not see himself as a martyr; he does not court death. But neither is his own suffering his only concern. His death is a cataclysmic event by which the world will pass judgment on itself. The critical time has arrived. Jesus prefaces his request with *if you are willing.* His first concern is for God's will, above his own desires. Jesus' prayer is not answered. He must drain the cup.

When Jesus finishes praying, he finds the disciples asleep, wakes them, and reiterates his instruction to pray for deliverance from the time of trial. When we compare Luke with Matthew and Mark, we find that his portrait of the disciples is more generous than that of the others (as is generally the case). Here the disciples fall asleep only once, and it is because of their *grief.* Jesus just tells them to get up and pray. None of the additional words in Matthew occur here.

## The "Missing" Verses

A word needs to be said about verses 43-44. In the NRSV these verses appear in brackets with a footnote reading, "Other ancient authorities lack verses 43 and 44." The RSV has these verses only in a footnote. The NEB includes them in the text. Since inclusion of the verses is debatable, different versions handle them in different ways. This means that several of the best and earliest copies of Luke do not have these verses. Remember that there are no originals of any book of the Bible. It is quite possible that these verses were added by a copyist in order to bring Luke closer to Matthew and Mark. As was noted above, without these two verses, the mood of the scene on the Mount of Olives is softened. One final note: verse 44b does not necessarily imply any miraculous event. It can simply mean that Jesus' sweat was so profuse it was as if he were bleeding sweat. Jesus' prayers are interrupted by the arrival of his enemies. It is to that final confrontation that we will next turn our attention.

## FOR FURTHER STUDY AND DISCUSSION

### Memory Bank

1. Luke 22:19, 20. The institution of the Lord's Supper.

**Research**

1. Ask your pastor about the origins of your denomination's understanding of the Lord's Supper. What aspects of Communion does your service of worship highlight? What do you understand to be happening during Communion?

2. Interview your pastor or ask for some reading material to explain why Communion is not a private affair.

**Reflection**

1. Read again Luke 22:14-23. What meaning does the Lord's Supper have for you? How do you understand the presence of Jesus Christ in this meal?

2. One of the classic definitions of sin is "self-centeredness." How do the disciples show that they are still in sin? For the next few days be conscious of how much of your thinking centers on your own wants and needs.

## SUMMARY

The authorities, accompanied by Judas, arrest Jesus on the Mount of Olives. He is taken to the home of the high priest for a hearing. Peter follows and there denies Jesus. Jesus is physically and verbally abused and brought before a council of Jewish leaders for questioning. The council takes Jesus to Pilate in order to have him tried, convicted, and executed by Rome. Pilate sends Jesus to Herod. Herod returns Jesus to Pilate. Pilate, at the urging of the Jewish authorities, condemns Jesus to death. Jesus is crucified with two others and dies. Joseph of Arimathea buries his body in a rock tomb. Women disciples from Galilee watch the burial and return home to prepare spices for the body and to observe the Sabbath.

## BASIC BIBLE REFERENCES

Luke 22:47-71
    23:1-56
Matthew 26:47-75
    27:1-2, 11-26, 32-61
Mark 14:43-72
    15:1-15, 21-47
John 18:3-40
    19:1-24, 28-42

## WORD LIST

Golgotha
Cyrene
Calvary
Paradise

*13*

# *The Passion Narrative (2)*

### *The Arrest of Jesus*

Read **Luke 22:47-53; also Matthew 26:47-56, Mark 14:43-52,** and **John 18:3-11**. The crowd that comes to arrest Jesus, is the same group of enemies who have sought his death since 19:47. They are headed by Judas. The kiss was a symbol of friendship. Only in Luke does Jesus prevent Judas from giving the kiss, as despicable an act as the betrayal itself. Judas is an enemy who tries to act like a friend.

One of the disciples who is a friend (identified as Peter in John's Gospel) acts like an enemy by trusting in violence to show his loyalty. Jesus calls a halt to violence on his behalf. Luke alone indicates that Jesus heals the injured man. Then Jesus addresses the hostile crowd, pointing out that their timing is consistent with their motives: since their deeds are evil, *the power of darkness* is their rightful ally.

### *Peter's Denial*

Continue with **Luke 22:54-62; also Matthew 26:69-75, Mark 14:66-72,** and **John 18:15-18, 25-27**. Jesus is brought that same night to the high priest's house. In Luke, Peter's denial takes place before the questioning of Jesus begins. Jesus' prediction about Peter's denial (22:31-34) comes true. (The strengthening of the other disciples will happen in Acts 1-5.)

Why was Peter there? What did he think he could do? He probably did not know. But he could not abandon Jesus–at least not unless his own safety was jeopardized. Three witnesses accuse Peter. Three times he denies Jesus. Only Luke mentions that after the cock crowed Jesus looked (presumably from a window) at Peter who was standing in the courtyard. Peter was overcome with remorse for what he had done, but not sufficiently so to turn and recant what he had said. With Peter's departure, Jesus is completely abandoned.

## *Jesus Is Mocked*

Now read **Luke 22:63-65;** also **Matthew 26:67-68,** and **Mark 14:65**. Jesus' reputation among the people as a prophet is the focus of his enemies' abuse. Jesus is not only kept up all night, but he is beaten. He is not accused of blasphemy, but Luke accuses Jesus' tormenters of blasphemy, for that is the Greek word he uses in verse 65 (translated *insults*). These verses must have been important to the church of Luke's day as it began to face persecutions. If Jesus could be treated this way because of his loyalty to God, certainly they could expect to be. Jesus set an example of how to bear indignities (see 1 Peter 2:21-23).

## *Jesus Before the Assembly*

At dawn Jesus is taken to an assembly of the Sanhedrin. Read **Luke 22:66-71;** also **Matthew 26:57-66, Mark 14:53-64,** and **John 18:12-14, 19-24**. They ask him two questions: whether he is the Messiah and whether he is the Son of God. To their demand about messiahship he replies that they are not looking for answers. They, in fact, only want statements to condemn him. He continues with an allusion to Daniel 7:13. Neither John nor Luke says that any charges about destroying the Temple were brought. No witnesses testify against Jesus. The leaders take Jesus' own words to be a claim that he is the Son of God. This would be blasphemy (unless it were true) although they do not use the word. Not everyone in Jesus' day was expecting a Messiah. Those who were did not always agree on what role he would play. The Messiah would not have been readily identified with the Son of God. Matthew and Mark, who put the two titles together, reflect the understanding of the later church. "Son of Man" was sometimes used as a messianic title, sometimes not. Jesus' response is ambiguous, but the authorities take it as affirmative.

## Jesus Before Pilate

Read **Luke 23:1-5;** also **Matthew 27:1-2, 11-14, Mark 15:1-5,** and **John 18:28-38.** All four Gospels agree that the Jewish authorities sent Jesus to Pilate, the Roman procurator of Judea. In fact, the council went with him. Before a Roman official a charge of blasphemy would be meaningless. The Romans had no interest in the theological debates of the Jews. When they cannot come up with a charge, Pilate tells them: *Take him yourselves and judge him according to your law* (John 18:31). Jesus' enemies need to find an offense that will stick in a Roman court. They come up with two: speaking out against paying imperial taxes and setting himself up as a king (a political rival to Caesar; see John 19:12). When Pilate asks about his kingship, Jesus answers in precisely the way he previously answered the Jewish leaders. The Jewish leaders take it as an admission of guilt; Pilate takes it to mean innocence.

Luke puts Rome in general and Pilate in particular in a more favorable light than do the other Gospels. He seems to be presenting a faith that has no interest in competing politically with Rome. In Luke and Acts, Roman officials are often portrayed sympathetically. Note that in Luke Pilate's soldiers do not abuse Jesus as they do in Matthew and Mark.

All four Gospels relate that Pilate saw no case for convicting Jesus of anything and, in effect, acquits Jesus: *I find no basis for an accusation against this man* (Luke 23:4). Yet Pilate is no hero. He is willing to transfer Jesus to Herod just to get rid of the problem, and he knowingly condemns an innocent man to death. Pilate himself is condemned out of his own mouth.

## Jesus Before Herod

Move on to **Luke 23:6-12.** This section is unique to Luke. Herod Antipas (the same Herod who had John the Baptizer beheaded) was technically a Jew but also a political puppet of the Roman Empire. He wants to be entertained by Jesus as if he were a magician. He questions Jesus at length, but Jesus refuses to speak. Jesus has made his opinion of Herod known before (13:32). Herod, tiring of the game which Jesus will not play, attempts to humiliate Jesus by dressing him in *an elegant robe.* (According to John 19:2b Pilate's soldiers put the robe on Jesus.) From Luke's point of view, the humiliation falls on the coarse and foolish Herod while Jesus retains all his dignity.

## Pilate Passes Sentence

Throughout the passion narrative Luke keeps responsibility for the death of Jesus on both Israel and Rome. There is no anti-Semitism here. The truth is that both Jews and Gentiles again and again rejected Jesus. No one group is singled out for blame. In Acts, Peter points out in his sermon at the Temple, *I know you acted in ignorance, as did also your rulers* in the death of Jesus (3:17). His sermon is designed to hold out forgiveness even in the face of the crucifixion.

Read **Luke 23:13-25;** also **Matthew 27:15-26, Mark 15:6-15,** and **John 18:39-19:16a**. Pilate, having received Jesus back from Herod, indicates that neither he nor Herod has any reason to convict Jesus of anything. When he seeks to placate the leaders by having Jesus scourged, Jesus' enemies know they have Pilate on the ropes.

Verse 17, missing in most of the earliest manuscripts (in NRSV it is a footnote), explains the custom of releasing a prisoner at the Passover. It was probably added to match Matthew's and Mark's explanations. Barabbas was a political prisoner. Pilate makes three attempts to release Jesus, but his enemies are insistent. The religious leaders threaten Pilate politically (John 19:12). The irony is complete. The religious leaders demand the death of God's Son while the heathen Gentile pleads his case. The Lord is condemned, and a murderer is released. This is as far from life in the kingdom as one could get.

## The Via Dolorosa[1]

Now read **Luke 23:26-31;** also **Matthew 27:32, Mark 15:21**. Only John does not mention Simon of Cyrene. Cyrene was the capital city of the North African district of Cyrenaica in the area of Libya. There were many people from that area in Jerusalem. There was a Cyrenian synagogue (Acts 6:9). Simon seems to have had nothing to do with the crucifixion except as a chance passerby whom the Romans pressed into service. The fact that Mark identifies him by his two sons, who were obviously known to his audience, has given rise to the idea that Simon and his family later became Christians.

The Romans usually made the condemned man carry his own cross—that is, the crossbeam. The vertical part of the cross would already be standing in the ground. The crossbeam would

---

1   The way of sorrow (Latin). A street in present-day Jerusalem is so named, and Jesus' sorrowful struggle is celebrated every Friday.

be carried over the shoulders like a yoke. Simon may have been forced to carry the cross-beam because Jesus, who had not slept since Wednesday and who had been whipped and beaten, could not manage it. The crowd that follows the procession to the place of execution is sympathetic to Jesus. Those who have been shouting against Jesus have been, for the most part, the religious leaders. Only in Luke does Jesus carry on a conversation with the crowds (6:27-31). Jesus responds to the women's outpouring of grief by warning them that they will soon be weeping for themselves. In that day children will be a burden as they flee Jerusalem. The picture is larger than it appears; Jesus is talking not only about his death but about the nation's demise.

## *The Crucifixion*

Turn to **Luke 23:32-44;** also **Matthew 27:33-44, Mark 15:22-32** and **John 19:16b-24**. Luke identifies the place of crucifixion as *the Skull*. In Hebrew skull is "Golgotha"; in Latin it is "Calvary." None of the Gospel writers speaks of the crucifixion as being on a hill.

All the Gospel writers agree that two others were crucified with Jesus. All agree that Jesus was on the center cross. Only Luke records the conversation with the dying thief who asked to be remembered by Jesus in the kingdom. Jesus' use of the word *paradise* is unusual. It is never used in the Old Testament and only in two other places in the New Testament (2 Corinthians 12:4 and Revelation 2:7). It is the abode of the righteous dead, an idea borrowed from the Persians. Most often life after death in the New Testament begins with the resurrection at the Judgment Day. The penitent thief is the kind of person who has been attracted to Jesus and the Gospel message throughout Luke. Even in his final hour, Jesus saves those for whom he came, although he will not call on the power of God to rescue himself from death.

In liturgical churches seven last words of Jesus have traditionally been read during Good Friday services. Matthew and Mark record only one word from the cross, *My God, my God, why have you forsaken me?* (Matthew 27:46; Mark 15:34b). John gives three statements and Luke the other three. *Father, forgive them; for they do not know what they are doing* is Luke's first. (It appears in brackets in the NRSV since it is found in only about half of the important copies of Luke. It is true to the spirit of Jesus and to the special interests of Luke's Gospel since forgiveness is a major theme.) "Them" in this brief prayer is most likely any and all who had to do with Jesus' death, Jew and Roman alike.

Jesus' last word from the cross (the second being the promise to the thief) is a shout or cry, *Father, into your hands I commend my spirit.* He is quoting Psalm 31:5. The word recorded by Matthew and Mark is also quoted from the Psalms (22:1a). Jesus puts his trust in God even in the face of death. This final word comes at about three in the afternoon. Luke does not tell us how long Jesus was on the cross. He mentions noon (23:44a) but not as a starting hour. Mark tells us that Jesus was crucified at nine in the morning and died at three.

## The Bystanders

Now read **Luke 23:35-49**[2]. Those gathered around the cross are mostly sympathetic to Jesus, at least in Luke. There are crowds present, but Luke singles out a number of bystanders. The religious leaders deride Jesus, apparently lecturing the crowds about him as if his death proves them right. In Matthew and Mark there are two attempts to give Jesus sour wine (vinegar). The first is wine mixed with gall or myrrh given, perhaps, to dull the pain. The second is the same as that recorded in Luke, given as part of the torture. The soldiers taunt Jesus about being "King of the Jews,"–the charge that is nailed above him on the cross. The unrepentant criminal throws the term "Messiah" at Jesus but of course does not believe it. The second criminal declares Jesus to be innocent. So does a centurion on guard duty at the site as he sees Jesus die. The crowds disperse, mourning in the traditional way, *beating their breasts.* This indicates that they regard Jesus' death not as justice but as a tragedy.

There is one other group in the scene that up to this point has not been mentioned: *the women who had followed him from Galilee.* We may assume that these are the women named in 8:1-3. They are the ones who will shortly prepare spices for Jesus' burial. Were any of these women among those original eyewitnesses (1:2)? The other three Gospels also give us a list of women present (Matthew 27:55-56, Mark 15:40-41, John 19:25). Mary Magdalene is on all the lists. Luke records no specific male disciples as having been present. He mentions a vague *all his acquaintances.* John's Gospel records the presence of the *disciple whom he loved* (19:26), into whose care Jesus gives his mother.

## Signs

Read again **Luke 23:44-49**; also **Matthew 27:45-56, Mark 15:33-41,** and **John 19:28-37**. Matthew, Mark and Luke record two unusual phenomena surrounding Jesus' death. *It was*

---

2  Occasionally there will be some overlap in the Basic Bible References.

*now about noon, and darkness came over the whole land until three in the afternoon, while the sun's light failed, and the curtain of the temple was torn in two* (Luke 23:44-45). Luke places together the darkness and the rending of the curtain, while Matthew and Mark tell us that the curtain was torn at the moment of Jesus' death.

The symbolism associated with darkness is obvious. It is literally "a dark day" not only for Jesus and his followers, but for "the whole land." Early manuscripts of Luke give several different versions of verse 45. In one the word for eclipse is used; in another the reading is "the sun having failed." An eclipse would have been impossible, for Passover takes place during a full moon when solar eclipses do not happen. No contemporary historians recorded an eclipse in the likely years. Neither Matthew nor Mark uses the word "eclipse." The later, traditional text reads "was darkened." What caused the darkness at noon is not Luke's concern; he would certainly have understood it to be a sign of God's great displeasure at what is taking place.

The second phenomenon is the tearing of the curtain of the Temple. It separated the Holy of Holies from the Holy Place, where the Ark of the Covenant resided. The Ark's presence was symbolic of the presence of God. The Holy of Holies was entered only once a year when the high priest offered sacrifice for the sins of the people. The Holy Place referred to the larger sanctuary area of the Temple. The tearing of the curtain is in the passive voice, "was torn," meaning that the action is God's. The placing of this incident at the instant of Jesus' death (Matthew and Mark) seems to indicate that precisely then God leaves the Temple; there is no longer any difference between the Holy Place and what used to be the Holy of Holies. In Ezekiel 10 the glory of the Lord left the Temple in anger and shortly after that the Temple was destroyed. For Mark and Matthew God has abandoned the Temple and Jerusalem. The nation's doom is sealed by the death of Jesus. It is significant that Luke has moved the rending of the curtain to a point before Jesus' death. For Luke the Temple had always been significant and would continue to be so until the end of the Gospel (24:53) and in the book of Acts, where the disciples continue to worship God in the Temple at Jerusalem (Acts 2:46). Luke is softening the symbolism of the curtain by placing it as he does. It is most certainly a negative symbol, and he combines it with the darkness at noon to assure that effect. But all is not yet lost. The people have acted in ignorance. Jesus on the cross has prayed for their forgiveness. The torn curtain is a warning, but not a symbol that the time for repentance is past.

## Jesus is Buried

Finally read **Luke 23:50-56;** also **Matthew 27:57-61, Mark 15:42-47,** and **John 19:38-42.** The description of the burial of Jesus begins with the introduction of a new figure, Joseph of Arimathea. Each Gospel writer adds something to the picture. Matthew tells us that he was a disciple of Jesus and a rich man; he had made the tomb. Mark informs us that Joseph was *a respected member of the council, who was also himself waiting expectantly for the kingdom of God.* He adds that Joseph's action of going right to Pilate to request Jesus' body was "bold." Joseph went and purchased the shroud in which he wrapped Jesus' body. John agrees with Matthew that Joseph was a disciple and adds, *though a secret one because of his fear of the Jews.* Only John tells us that Joseph had an ally in the work, Nicodemus, another member of the Sanhedrin, who had earlier come to Jesus by night to ask how to be born anew. Luke holds Joseph in high regard, telling us that he was *good and righteous,* that he had not agreed with the other members of the Sanhedrin. He repeats Matthew's words that Joseph was *waiting expectantly for the kingdom of God.* This description is very similar to the way in which Luke described Simeon (2:25), a man who spoke by the power of the Holy Spirit. Joseph of Arimathea acts with great courage, for his request for Jesus' body would almost surely reveal him to Pilate as a disciple or a sympathizer. Members of the Sanhedrin would naturally want the body removed before the Sabbath began, but this is not Joseph's motivation. Joseph honors the Lord in the most practical of ways, giving him the final dignity which both Rome and the Jewish Law would usually deny a crucified criminal. Joseph, having rendered to Jesus the only service he could, is heard from in the Gospels no more.

The tomb in which Jesus' body is laid is a new one, never used, pure and appropriate for holy use, much as the colt he rode when he entered Jerusalem. The tomb has been carved ("hewn") out of a cliff or hillside; it is not a naturally occurring cave. Israel has precious little good land; it is not often used for burials. Several types of vaults were used in Jesus' day, but none of the Gospel writers is very specific as to which kind was used in Jesus' case. However, there is enough here and in descriptions in the Easter narratives to suggest a type with a sizable room having shelves about two feet wide on which bodies would be laid. The entrance would be sealed with a large boulder. In more elaborate burial caves, a dressed boulder would slide into place along a trough carved into the front entrance. Luke does not mention the boulder across the entrance until the resurrection scene in 24:2.

Matthew, Mark, and Luke all write that women disciples were present at the burial, watching Joseph work. They were not weeping and wailing as was the custom, but, probably exhausted, they simply sat in stunned silence. They wanted to be sure that their Lord's body was being cared for. Matthew and Mark name the women: Mary Magdalene and another Mary. Luke refers to them as *the women who had come with him from Galilee.*

There is haste involved in the burial efforts, for it was the day of Preparation, the day before the Sabbath. And it was nearing sundown, the beginning of the Sabbath. The Jews reckoned days from sundown to sundown. The women, then, cannot prepare the body with fragrant oils and spices, but return home to get them ready and to observe the Sabbath rest, obedient as always to Jewish practices.

## FOR FURTHER STUDY AND DISCUSSION

### Memory Bank

1. Memorize the seven words from the cross: Luke 23:34, 43, 46; Matthew 27:46; John 19:26-27, 28, 30.

### Research

1. Read about "crucifixion" in a reference book.

2. A constant theme in the ministry of Jesus is "reversal." What reversal takes place in the crucifixion?

### Reflection

1. Luke shows Pilate as a man caught "between a rock and a hard place." Pilate sold out justice to protect his job. How would you have fared in Pilate's place? Have you ever sold out the truth for short-term security?

## SUMMARY

The women who had watched Joseph of Arimathea bury Jesus' body return immediately as the Sabbath ends to finish burial preparations. They find the tomb empty. Two men inform them that Jesus is alive. The women tell this to the apostles and to those gathered with them, but the assembly does not believe them. Two disciples meet the risen Jesus on the road to Emmaus. These disciples return to Jerusalem to report what has happened and are informed that there has been an appearance to Simon as well. As they are discussing this, Jesus stands among them. He leads them to Bethany, where he ascends. After this the disciples spend their days in Jerusalem, specifically at the Temple waiting for the coming of the Spirit.

## BASIC BIBLE REFERENCES

Luke 24 :1-53
Matthew 28:1-8, 16-20
Mark 16:1-8
John 20 :1-10, 19-23
1 Corinthians 15:3-8

## WORD LIST

ascension

# *The Resurrection*

## Women's Work

Read **Luke 24:1-12;** also **Matthew 28:1-8, Mark 16:1-8** and **John 20:1-10**. The Sabbath ends at sundown on Saturday. On the first day of the week the women come as soon as it is light enough to finish the work they could not finish on Friday evening. *They* in Luke 24:1 refers to the women from Galilee (23:49, 55) who were present at the crucifixion and the burial. Matthew and Mark had named two of the women who saw the burial: *Mary Magdalene, and Mary the mother of James the younger and of Joses* (Mark 15:40). Matthew calls her the other Mary (27:61b). Luke supplies an additional name, Joanna. Mark adds Salome. Luke tells us that there were *other women with them.* Only John tells us that Mary Magdalene apparently came alone. Luke says the women came with spices and were met by an open tomb. They enter the tomb and find the body gone. While they are trying to figure out what happened *two men in dazzling clothes* appear and stand beside them. These men are later identified as "angels." John and Luke mention two angels; Matthew and Mark mention one. All are reported to be in shining or white garments.

## The Angels' Message

The message of resurrection is stated clearly to the terrified women: *Why do you look for the living among the dead? He is not here, but has risen.* The messengers remind the women of Jesus' prophecy made in Galilee (9:22). Matthew and Mark relate the message to go to Galilee. Luke tells only about resurrection appearances in the vicinity of Jerusalem, the city which will continue in Acts to be the focus of the church's activity. It is in Jerusalem that the disciples will receive the Holy Spirit (Acts 2) and it is from Jerusalem that the Gospel will be sent into all the world.

The angels' message contains a statement which was one of the earliest creeds of the Christian Church: *that the Son of Man must be handed over to sinners, and be crucified, and on the third day rise again.* Paul, writing before the composition of the Gospels, has much the same statement; read **1 Corinthians 15:3-4**. This is the bedrock affirmation of the Christian faith, and Luke will leave his readers with no uncertainty about it.

The women *remembered his words.* According to Luke these words were said *when Jesus was praying alone, with only the disciples near him* (9:18-21). These women, then, may have been members of Jesus' inner circle, not just part of the wider crowd of disciples.

## The Empty Tomb

All four Gospels report that the tomb of Jesus was empty at sunrise on Sunday morning. Luke underlines the significance of this fact by repeating it in the Emmaus road story (see below) and by confirming it in verse 24 with an incident he did not record before. Peter himself makes a trip to the tomb and finds it empty. Writers often repeat what they have already written in order to underscore the truth or importance of an event. Luke uses this device many times. The point of the empty tomb is to allow no other interpretation of the events except that the Jesus who was crucified, dead, and buried is the same as the Christ who was resurrected. There can be no confusion on that point: *Look at my hands and my feet; see that it is I myself. Touch me, and see* (24:39). This is not some subjective, mystical, or interpretive idea about Jesus. The body that was buried is recognized in the resurrection.

## The Disciples React

The women's message (the preaching of the first Easter sermon) is met, not surprisingly, with disbelief by the *eleven* and *all the rest.* Luke consistently relates that there are more people involved here than just the eleven disciples and the women from Galilee. Who would believe such a story second hand? Peter goes so far as to make a trip to the tomb, but his reaction is not clear. Luke only says he was *amazed at what had happened,* which at this point only seems to mean the disappearance of Jesus' body.

## The Walk to Emmaus

Only Luke tells about the walk to Emmaus. Read **24:13-27**. This event occurs on Easter day, late in the afternoon. Two disciples are involved, one is never named; the other, Cleopas, appears nowhere else. The two are quite naturally discussing all that has happened over the weekend: the crucifixion of their Lord and the strange story they have heard this morning from the women. These two must have been with *all the rest* mentioned in verse 9.

Jesus appears to them as they walk down the road, but *their eyes were kept from recognizing him.* Luke has told before of instances where understanding is withheld (for example, see 9:45). The passive voice indicates that the action is God's. The resurrected Christ will be known only by revelation. Jesus asks them what they have been discussing, and with sadness Cleopas begins the painful chore of listing all that has happened. He refers to Jesus as *a prophet mighty in deed and word before God and all the people.* The events of the last few days cannot change that. For Cleopas Jesus had indeed been a prophet of God. However the crucifixion had changed another of Cleopas' beliefs: *But we had hoped that he was the one to redeem Israel,* that is, the Messiah. For Cleopas, Jesus' death had destroyed any possibility that he could have been God's Messiah.

As on other occasions Jesus is frustrated with his own disciples' inability to trust the promises of God. All the promises to Israel are fulfilled in these events. From beginning to end the Gospel of Luke declares over and over that Jesus is the culmination of all the promises of the Old Testament. In verse 26 Jesus speaks of the necessity of the Messiah's suffering. The Jews had no such concept; in fact the idea of a suffering Messiah would have seemed to them a contradiction in terms. Jesus reinterprets *Moses and all the prophets,* that is, the Hebrew Scriptures, in order to show how his life, death, and resurrection bring God's promises to fruition. Again, this knowledge comes by divine revelation.

## Known in Breaking Bread

Now read **24:28-35**. The disciples reach their destination, but Jesus walks on ahead as if to continue his journey. He comes into the disciple's house only by a very sincere invitation; *they urged him strongly.* It may be that Luke has here a message for all who would know

Jesus: the first step is a real and convincing invitation. It is significant that Jesus is a guest who takes the role of the host. It is he who *took bread, blessed and broke it, and gave it to them.* The language Luke uses here to describe this event is deliberately that of Holy Communion (see 1 Corinthians 11:23-26).

The minds of the two disciples have been opened to know Christ in the Scriptures, and now they will know him in the sacramental *breaking of the bread.* When Jesus breaks the bread, the disciples are allowed to recognize him. Here again Luke has a message for the church. Christ is experienced in the Word and Sacrament; by these, disciples come into Christ's presence firsthand. No matter how many or how sincere the words of witnesses may be, Christian faith finally depends on each person meeting Jesus Christ firsthand. The faith of a Christian must always be in God, not in the trust one has in others. Luke tells us that the Scriptures and the sacraments open a way to this encounter. This sacramental meal is a celebration of resurrection and of the presence of God, who in the raising of Jesus from the dead has declared forgiveness and victory over death.

Jesus disappears, and the disciples are left to figure out what has happened. When the women encountered the empty tomb, they were told to remember what Jesus had said. That memory helped them to understand the truth of what they had encountered. The same is true for Cleopas and his friend. They had heard the words of Jesus and then encountered him in the breaking of the bread. Now they can put it all together: *Were not our hearts burning within us while he was talking to us on the road, while he was opening the scriptures to us?* The church remembers Jesus' words and all the words of Scripture in order to understand who has been encountered. We read and hear the Scriptures first. When we meet God in our lives, then we can recognize whom we are encountering. We do not believe in God because we believe in the Scriptures; we believe in the Scriptures because we have encountered the God of whom they speak. When Jesus was revealed to the two disciples in the breaking of the bread, the words of Scripture helped them to make sense of the encounter.

The Emmaus travelers respond to meeting the risen Christ by bearing witness, sharing what has happened. That very night they return to Jerusalem to report to the apostles and those with them. Their story, however, is scooped, for they are met with the words, *The Lord has risen indeed, and he has appeared to Simon.* (Could it be that Simon, after the events of Thursday night, can no longer bear to be called "Rock"?)

This appearance to Simon Peter would make him the first to actually see the resurrected Lord. Paul indicates that this is the case; read **1 Corinthians 15:5-8**. ("Cephas" is the Hebrew form of "Peter"; both words mean "rock.") Matthew and John indicate that Mary Magdalene was the first to see the resurrected Christ (in Matthew the other women are included). This discrepancy was not a problem for the early church; they tended to tie all resurrection appearances together. Luke's interest here is not in chronology but in the resurrection of Jesus from the dead and his appearance to his own.

Note that the two disciples did not run out into the streets to declare the resurrection. They went rather to the other believers. The courage and power that they will need to proclaim the gospel to those who have not seen will come when the Holy Spirit is given to them. They repeat that Christ was known to them *in the breaking of the bread.*

## Jesus Appears

Turn to **Luke 24:36-43**; also **John 20:19-23**. Luke and John provide the majority of resurrection appearance stories. Matthew has only two: the women as they run from the tomb and the eleven at the ascension. The original end of Mark's Gospel is missing; hence there are no resurrection appearances. (The additional material in Mark–everything after 16:8–was added by later scribes.) Both Luke and John report an appearance by Jesus to the disciples on Easter evening. In both reports Jesus enters the room suddenly. In John's version he appears even though the doors are locked. Luke as well understands Jesus' entrance to be miraculous. Jesus shows his wounded hands and feet to the disciples to prove that it really is he, and the disciples rejoice. In John's version the disciples receive the Holy Spirit and the power to forgive sins, but Luke describes the giving of the Holy Spirit in Acts 2.

Luke, more than the other Gospels, deals with the nature of Christ's resurrected body. Jesus vanishes and appears apparently at will. Yet he eats a piece of broiled fish in order to show that he is quite real and invites the terrified disciples to touch him to prove that he is not a ghost: *Touch me and see; for a ghost does not have flesh and bones as you see that I have* (24:39). Jesus makes much the same offer to doubting Thomas in John 20:27. In Luke all the disciples seem to have a great deal of trouble believing. They are afraid that they are dealing with the dead (a ghost or spirit). Jesus assures them that he is bodily alive. This is again a repeated message. The angel first proclaimed it at the tomb. The resurrection is not some vision of the dead, but a reality.

With what kind of body then are the dead raised?[1] Luke does not attempt to answer such a question. He simply bears witness to what has happened. He puts stories of miraculous comings and goings side by side with Jesus' claims to be flesh and blood. John does the same. Luke and John are theologians, not philosophers. The task of philosophy is to talk about what could be or should be. The task of Christian theology is to bear witness to what God has done. The body of the resurrected Christ is identified with the body that was crucified; the wounds are still there. The Jesus who ate with sinners, cured the ill, raised the dead, and called the disciples is the same Jesus who is now, by God's power, the resurrected Christ. Luke, along with all the Gospel writers, goes to great lengths to make that perfectly clear. There is no idea here of some immortal soul that lives on after death. The Jews had no conception of any such thing (see Part 11). The Jesus who stands before them has died and been raised from death by the supreme power of the only God.

## Marching Orders

Read **Luke 24:44-49;** also **Matthew 28:16-20.** In Luke Jesus reminds the disciples that what has happened is precisely what he said would happen. It has been God's purpose all along, as the Scriptures of the Old Testament attest. Again, knowledge of Jesus comes through revelation as *he opened their minds to understand the scriptures.* The message is the same as that given to Cleopas and his friend on the Emmaus road.

Luke 24:47 adds to that message a commission to Jesus' followers. In Matthew's Gospel the commission has the same charge to take the Gospel to *all nations (ethne* in the Greek, which also can mean "Gentiles"). In Luke Jesus specifies that repentance and forgiveness, two of Luke's major themes, are to be proclaimed to all nations in Christ's name. The mission is to begin in Jerusalem. The commencement of that mission is the story Luke tells in Acts. The charge to proclaim repentance and God's love to all nations is not new. It has been God's purpose from the beginning of the salvation story. It is as old as Abraham (Genesis 18:18) and the great prophet Isaiah (60:3). In Jesus Christ the whole world is called to repentance for the sake of being forgiven.

The apostles are to be *witnesses,* that is those who give testimony to what they have seen and heard. In Greek the word is *martys* from which we get the word "martyr." So many Christians died because of their witness for Christ that the word came to mean one who

---

1   This question was put to Paul, who gives his response in 1 Corinthians 15:35-49.

dies for the faith. In Acts many of Jesus' disciples died a martyr's death. They would accept death rather than deny their Lord. A Christian is not a pampered favorite of God but a witness to the truth of God's love and forgiveness as it is experienced in Jesus Christ. If such a witness brings death, that is acceptable. Jesus' final words in Matthew are a promise to be with the believers. Luke has the same promise; Jesus says that it is a promise from *my Father:* that his disciples will be *clothed with power from on high.* That power is the Holy Spirit, which will reside in the Christian community, giving it the ability to fulfil its commission to take the Gospel into the whole world.

## *The Ascension*

Finally, read **Luke 24:50-53**. The ascension is repeated in Acts 1:6-11 in a fuller form. In the Gospel this shorter version perhaps provides a complete unit for Easter worship in the church. Everything in chapter 24 happens on Easter day and night–Luke has tended to lump it all together. But Luke himself states in Acts 1:3 that appearances continued for *forty days* and that the ascension took place after that.

The ascension symbolizes the glorification of Jesus, who has completed his work and will return in the power of the Holy Spirit. Luke's Gospel ends as it begins, in the Temple at Jerusalem, where God is continually worshiped by the disciples of Jesus.

## FOR FURTHER STUDY AND DISCUSSION

### Memory Bank

1. Luke 24:5-7. The angels' procamation to the women.

2. 24:46-49. Jesus' proclamation to all the disciples.

### Research

1. Read several Easter hymns. What does resurrection mean for the hymn writers? What does the resurrection of Jesus mean for you?

2. Use a concordance to locate several references to resurrection in the New Testament. Write a statement about the meaning of resurrection for Jesus Christ, for individuals, and for the church.

## Reflection

1. How does the Emmaus road story change the mood of Holy Communion for you? Is a change of mood needed in your church's celebration of Holy Communion? What would facilitate a change? How does "solemn" avoid becoming "somber"?

2. Read Paul's words in 1 Corinthians 15:17. How does the entire Christian faith hinge on the resurrection of Jesus Christ? How do you understand the importance of the resurrection?

3. List specific ways that you and your congregation are living out the commission in Luke 24:47, 48.